Religion in America: A Very Short Introduction

VERY SHORT INTRODUCTIONS are for anyone wanting a stimulating and accessible way in to a new subject. They are written by experts, and have been published in more than 25 languages worldwide.

The series began in 1995, and now represents a wide variety of topics in history, philosophy, religion, science, and the humanities. Over the next few years it will grow to a library of around 200 volumes — a Very Short Introduction to everything from ancient Egypt and Indian philosophy to conceptual art and cosmology.

Very Short Introductions available now:

For more information visit our web site
www.oup.co.uk/general/vsi/

Timothy Beal

RELIGION IN AMERICA

A Very Short Introduction

OXFORD
UNIVERSITY PRESS

OXFORD
UNIVERSITY PRESS

Oxford University Press, Inc., publishes works that further
Oxford University's objective of excellence
in research, scholarship, and education.

Oxford   New York
Auckland   Cape Town   Dar es Salaam   Hong Kong   Karachi
Kuala Lumpur   Madrid   Melbourne   Mexico City   Nairobi
New Delhi   Shanghai   Taipei   Toronto

With offices in
Argentina   Austria   Brazil   Chile   Czech Republic   France   Greece
Guatemala   Hungary   Italy   Japan   Poland   Portugal   Singapore
South Korea   Switzerland   Thailand   Turkey   Ukraine   Vietnam

Published by Oxford University Press, Inc.
198 Madison Avenue, New York, NY 10016

www.oup.com

Oxford is a registered trademark of Oxford University Press

Library of Congress Cataloging-in-Publication Data
Beal, Timothy K. (Timothy Kandler), 1963-
Religion in America : a very short introduction / Timothy Beal.
p. cm.— (Very short introductions; 184)
Includes bibliographical references and index.
ISBN 978-0-19-532107-4 (pbk.)
1. United States—Religion. I. Title.
BL2525.B395 2008
200.973—dc22
2007047153

1   3   5   7   9   8   6   4   2

Printed in the United States of America
on acid-free paper

to my beloved daughter and son

Sophie
&
Seth

with gratitude for insight,
humor, perspective

Contents

List of Illustrations

Acknowledgments

Writing a very short introduction to a very huge subject like religion in America is very hard in ways very different from any other project I've undertaken. I have been most grateful to my editor, Cybele Tom, for her guidance and careful, critical attention to my work throughout the research and writing process, and to Mary Sutherland for outstanding copyediting. I also thank Elda Rotor, the editor who first approached me about writing this book.

Several people have offered direction, background, and critical feedback at various points along the way. I am especially grateful to the three anonymous readers for their comments and suggestions, to Geraldine Beal, maternal copyeditor, and to many generous colleagues, especially Joy Bostic, William E. Deal, Ed Gemerchak, Peter Haas, Tod Linafelt, Vincent Miller, S. Brent Plate, Ted Steinberg, fellow members of the Baker-Nord Seminars on "Homelands and Security" (2004) and "Information" (2006), the student colleagues in my 2003 Senior Seminar who helped carry out the Case Pluralism Project, and Tell Mac in Diaspora. Many thanks as well to Hannah Whitehead for excellent research assistance on chapter 2, especially in sorting out the statistical data and drawing (and pruning!) the family tree illustration.

I have benefited greatly from the work of several scholars of religion in America, and I gladly acknowledge some of the most influential ones here: Catherine L. Albanese, Randall Balmer, Vine Deloria, Diana L. Eck, Martin E. Marty, Stephen Prothero, Robert Orsi, and Stephen J. Stein.

Finally, and as ever, I am most grateful to my family: to Clover for loving encouragement, collegial conversation, and mindful discernment; and to our kids, Seth and Sophie, who remind me daily, when I have ears to hear and eyes to see, not to take myself too seriously.

Introduction

One Sunday Morning

As I begin writing this introduction to a very short introduction to religion in America, it's Sunday morning and I'm sitting in a fine example of a very American institution, the breakfast diner. In an hour or so I'll go to another very American institution, a Presbyterian church, where my wife is a minister. I've just finished picking up several dozen donuts and delivering them to the fellowship hall there. (I wonder how many members we'd lose if we stopped serving donuts before services!) There's no Sunday school this morning, so I have an hour before I need to pick up our kids and get back to church with them in time for worship.

There was a time in America, not very long ago, even in a city like Cleveland, when I would've been hard pressed to find a diner open on Sunday, the implicit message being that everyone should be in church. That's still the case in some small towns, especially in the South and Midwest. But for many today, breakfast and a newspaper in a diner *is* church.

In the *New York Times* this morning: debates over a Senate bill to overhaul immigration; a review of a book about how James Dobson, founder and head of the conservative evangelical organization Focus on the Family, is fighting and winning the culture wars. Among this week's nonfiction best sellers: a book about the Buddha by Deepak Chopra; *Eat, Pray, Love,* a memoir of spiritual awakening by Elizabeth Gilbert; a new translation of Elie Wiesel's Holocaust survival narrative, *Night*; *Reposition Yourself,* a book of spiritual guidance by the famous African American minister T. D. Jakes; and this spring's big hit, *God Is Not Great: How Religion Poisons Everything,* by Christopher Hitchens, which is following close on the heels of other best-selling broadsides on religious people and beliefs by Richard Dawkins (*The God Delusion*) and Sam Harris (*Letter to a Christian Nation*).

The diner's big screen TV is tuned to CNN Headline News. Among this morning's top stories, constantly interrupted by ads for lawn and barbeque products, fast food, and cars: eulogistic recollections of Jerry Falwell, founder of the Moral Majority in the late 1970s and leader of the so-called Christian Right, who died almost two weeks ago; a legal controversy over the use of the Qur'an by Muslims for swearing to tell the truth and nothing but the truth in North Carolina courts of law (a group of Muslims had tried to donate copies to Guilford County's two courthouses, and the two judges rejected them, leading to a Supreme Court decision to allow a witness to swear on whatever text is most sacred to her or him); a twenty-seven-year-old American citizen extradited from the United Kingdom to the United States to face charges of supporting Al Qaeda; dozens of American flags in a graveyard on Orcas Island, Washington, removed from veterans' graves, burned, and replaced with paper drawings of swastikas; the Bush administration's reiteration, in characteristically religious terms, of its commitment to the war in Iraq, so that the sacrifices of those who have died fighting against the evils of terror will not be for naught.

It's Memorial Day weekend. For many Americans, if not for the neo-Nazi flag-burners of Orcas Island, tomorrow will be honored as a quasi-religious holiday dedicated to sanctifying the memory of those who have died at war while serving in the nation's military.

Most conservative evangelical Christian churches will recognize Memorial Day in worship services today. Indeed, many such churches will observe it as a high holy day.

Today is also Pentecost Sunday, a Christian holiday second only to Easter in significance within the church calendar of Sundays. On Pentecost Sunday, congregations around the world celebrate the birth of the church, as told in the second chapter of the New Testament book of Acts, when cloven tongues of fire descended on the apostles; they were filled with the Holy Spirit and began speaking in foreign tongues. This story is also where that uniquely homegrown American form of Christianity, Pentecostalism, gets its name. Its genesis a century ago among a racially and economically mixed group of women and men meeting in a house on Azusa Street in Los Angeles is remembered as another Pentecost, in which many people received the spiritual gift of *glossolalia*, speaking in unknown tongues.

This morning in our reserved, liberal-intellectual Presbyterian church, some of us might clap our hands to a gospel song. The choir will perform a multilingual, dramatic reading of the second chapter of Acts. And we'll have a jazz band accompanying our hymn singing. But we won't be nearly so wildly Pentecostal as they will be in the charismatic African American church up the road. They don't call Presbyterians "the frozen chosen" for nothing. Indeed, an outside observer would be forgiven for wondering if our church and the one up the road are even part of the same religion.

Rarely do Pentecost Sunday and Memorial Day weekend coincide. When they do, they create a political and cultural watershed among Christian communities concerning the relationship between religion and nationalism, with so-called conservative and fundamentalist churches falling out on one side and so-called liberal and progressive churches on the other. This morning, many conservative churches will honor Memorial Day in prayer and song and sermon far more than they will Pentecost Sunday. In more liberal and radical Christian churches, on the other hand, where there is much concern about compromising biblical values of social justice, locally and globally, by state interests and power politics, Memorial Day is believed to have little or no place in worship—except as an opportunity to recognize the tragic losses of war, "ours" and "theirs" alike. In our church, with a majority of liberals, a few radicals, and a few conservatives, we'll see a strong lean toward the latter approach to Memorial Day with a nod to those who wish it were honored more centrally: a patriotic hymn, perhaps, or a somber acknowledgment of congregation members who are veterans or who have lost loved ones to war. So too the church up the road, where many congregation members have sons and spouses and friends who are serving or have been killed or wounded in Iraq.

A few blocks farther up the road, Orthodox Jewish families dressed in black are talking and laughing as they walk to their synagogues for Sunday classes. I don't imagine Memorial Day will be a prominent theme in their Torah study this morning. Pentecost certainly won't.

A way in

So it's an auspicious Sunday morning to be writing an introduction to religion in America, a topic that inevitably involves matters of church and state, God and country. If an anthropologist from Mars were to spend only this weekend in America, she'd get more than a very short introduction to the topic. Among her notes might be the following:

predominantly Christian, more specifically Protestant, with the most vocal majority being theologically conservative and evangelical; yet, despite many representations in the media, there is tremendous diversity within Christianity in America, from Pentecostals to nondenominational megachurches to Roman Catholics to the old mainstream Protestant traditions like

4

Presbyterians and Methodists (which are shrinking in membership with every passing year) to radical militant groups like Christian Identity with neo-Nazi sympathies; divisions and segregations by race and class; major disagreements on central matters both doctrinal and political to such an extent that it might make more sense to talk about *Christianities* rather than Christianity in America; and although the country remains predominantly Christian, other minority religions have a powerful social and cultural presence; some, like Judaism, have long been part of the American religious landscape, going all the way back to the colonial period, despite a long history of anti-Jewish prejudice and persecution; other religious groups, including Muslims, Buddhists, Jains, and Hindus, are growing rapidly, and their presence is beginning to be felt more strongly in the public sphere; it seems that the fastest growing population is that of people who do not identify with any religion; among religious people, especially conservative Christians, there is general tendency toward nationalism and an almost religious reverence for war, which is often sanctified in political rhetoric through the language of sacrifice and the battle of good against evil; at the same time, there is a growing interreligious countermovement of people who believe that their various religious convictions call them to struggle against nationalism and war; within the various religious traditions we find core values of care and hospitality toward the stranger . . . and we find fear of the stranger.

The religious landscape of America is not as simple or uniform as it might initially appear. Indeed, it's hard to think of a single aspect of American culture, past or present, in which religion has not played a major part. The parts it plays, moreover, appear to be growing more bewilderingly complex and diverse every day.

Many people want a fuller and deeper understanding of the current realities and historical backgrounds of religion in America. Yet they're at a loss for where to begin. I hope that this book will provide a good point of entry. Written with nonspecialists and students in mind, I mean to offer an accessible way in to the broad range of topics and issues concerning religion in America, past and present.

Overview

In any introduction, there is a risk of overgeneralizing, of ignoring those particulars that don't fit with the big picture. Yet the heart of any religious belief, practice, or institution is in the details. In this book, we'll try to avoid this hazard by moving back and forth between the general and the particular, the big picture and local snapshots.

Many of us know more about religion in America in general than we do about the rich diversity of religious communities in our own neighborhoods. We begin not with the big picture but with a personal introduction, which briefly explores two very local religious landscapes: first, my daily ten-minute commute, which takes me past more than fifty religious landmarks, churches, synagogues, mosques, temples, monasteries, schools, and community centers; and second, my own campus community, which is growing more religiously diverse every year. While each of these local landscapes is absolutely unique in many respects, I suggest that each is also, at the same time, something of a microcosm of religion in America.

With these local landscapes in mind, we step back to get the really big picture—a satellite's eye view of the American religious landscape. First, we'll consider the numbers according to the most reliable polling data. How many Buddhists are there in America today? How many Pentecostals? Which populations are growing? Which are shrinking? Next, we'll consider those elements of religion in America that are not so easily measured in statistics. For example, we'll consider a few examples of new religious movements, or NRMs, which have always been a part of the American religious landscape but which appear to be emerging more frequently over the past several decades. We'll also look at "outsider religion," a term I use for those mavericks whose highly individual religious identities take form far outside the mainstreams of society. Finally, we'll consider the powerful influence of religion in the public spheres of politics and popular culture.

E Pluribus Unum, "from many, one." By the end of this book, we begin to recognize that this motto from the Great Seal of the United States represents not only a great American ideal but also an abiding paradox that goes to the very heart of religion in America: an affirmation of *both* the *one* and the *many*, of unity and plurality, of collective identity and individual difference, of conformity and dissent. On the one hand, America is rich in highly particular, often highly peculiar religious groups and individuals. On the other hand, running counter to this proliferation of the religiously peculiar and particular, we are all very aware of the predominance of Christian beliefs and values, especially Protestant ones, in American society and culture. What makes the American *terra religiosa* such fertile ground for this paradox? This is our central question in the chapters that follow, as we consider past and present influences.

After gaining a fuller, richer sense of the big picture of religion in America today, we'll try to gain some historical perspective on how this fascinating religious landscape has taken shape. Mind, this is not an introduction to the history of religion in America. (Please see my bibliography for recommended further reading in American religious history.) Nor do I presume that there can be any such thing as a single, unifying story of religion in America. There is no such thing. There is no grand narrative, no march of progress, or of devolution for that matter. Nonetheless, historical perspective can shed light on certain issues that remain central when it comes to religion in America today. In this chapter, we look back into American religious history and draw out three especially formative historical influences: the colonization of America and the dispossession of Native Americans; the struggle for religious freedom and the First Amendment; and the history of revivalism, which has given rise to a uniquely American evangelical consciousness.

Next, we consider current forces of social change that are impacting religion in America today: the rise of religious diversity in America, the rise of the information society, and the rise of consumer culture. These are not independent forces but are integrally related to one another. Taken separately, their influence on the religious landscape of America would be great enough; taken together, their influence will be exponentially greater, radically changing that landscape in yet unimaginable ways.

Finally, we return to the paradox so succinctly captured in the motto, *E Pluribus Unum*. Here the paradox of the one and the many becomes a dilemma: how can a nation or society achieve a sense of unity and identity without eradicating differences and enforcing homogeneity, religious or otherwise? How to avoid, as Martin E. Marty puts it, "forcing one story on the many." In his now classic *Democracy in America*, the early nineteenth-century French philosopher and American pilgrim Alexis de Tocqueville asked this question. Today, Americans continue to grapple with it, albeit not always consciously. As simple as it is difficult, the way forward calls for a commitment to making space in our hearts, homes, cities, and nation for interreligious dialogue. To quote Marty again: "start associating, telling, hearing, and keep talking."

The book opens with local neighborhood snapshots of religion in an old American city, so it seems appropriate to close with a brief trip to the woods. We'll visit the Furnace Mountain Zen Buddhist temple and retreat center in the Daniel Boone National Forest in eastern Kentucky—very near Cane Ridge, where the Second Great Awakening began more than two centuries ago. As we'll see, Cane Ridge and Furnace Mountain have more in common than we might initially expect.

Hospitality and security

How can a nation or society achieve a sense of unity and identity without eradicating differences and enforcing homogeneity, religious or otherwise? This is not only a political or social challenge; it is an ethical dilemma. Today, in a post-9/11, post-traumatic America, fraught with anxieties about its changing role in the world, exhausted and despairing from a seemingly endless "war on terror," I suggest the ethical import of this dilemma is one of *hospitality versus security*.

By hospitality, I mean openness to the other, that is, to any person or idea that is foreign, unknown, strange to me or "us." Hospitality is about letting the other into one's home, one's family, one's heart and mind. It is about being open to a relationship with otherness.

Hospitality, in this sense, is risky. It is a threat to security—physical security, financial security, domestic security, national security, and even intellectual and spiritual security. For security is grounded in a sense of unity, a feeling that there is no threat of invasion from "outside." Security guards against otherness.

The dilemma of hospitality versus security runs through every nook and cranny of American society, from the ways we relate (or don't relate) to others in our neighborhoods and cities to the ways the government legislates immigration and gathers intelligence. From the shopping mall to the National Mall. From the fences in our backyards to the proposed fence along the Mexican border. From home security systems to the Department of Homeland Security.

As a doctoral student in the early 1990s, I spent a summer working on an archeological excavation in southern Jordan. The site of the dig was in the small town of South Shuna, just across the Jordan River valley from the site of ancient Jericho. The region was heavily populated with Palestinian refugees. People were constantly aware of tensions with Israel, whose borders were visible beyond the guard stations in the valley.

Yet, despite this sense of border insecurity, and despite being heavily burdened with refugees from another land, the local Jordanians were the most hospitable people I'd ever encountered. I was repeatedly overwhelmed by their welcoming openness. In South Shuna and in the nearby town of Deir Alla where we camped (alleged to be the spot where the biblical brothers Jacob and Esau reconciled), people would come out of their homes to greet us and invite us to dinner. If they had but one chicken, they'd happily cook it up for us, with no expectation of anything in return. Within that culture, a very high value is placed on hospitality, even at the risk of security, financial and otherwise.

On my return flight, there were several Jordanian families coming to the United States on vacation. Their excitement was palpable: parents chatting happily while kids ran up and down the aisles wearing Mickey Mouse ears and Little Mermaid T-shirts. As I watched them, I felt more than a tinge of sadness. I imagined that they imagined that they might be welcomed with the same kind of hospitality that they would show anyone on vacation in their country. I imagined they would be disappointed.

That was the summer of 1992, almost a decade before the attacks of September 11, 2001. In their aftermath, the dilemma of hospitality versus security is all the more acute. Too often, tragically, we are foregoing hospitality for the sake of security, even for the sake of the illusion of security. *Hospitality v. security.*

If the icon of American hospitality is the Statue of Liberty on Liberty Island, the icon of insecurity is the blank space on the Manhattan skyline where the World Trade Center's twin towers once stood.

A true dilemma is ultimately not resolvable; you can't just choose one of its horns and lop off the other. Hospitality versus security is a true ethical dilemma. It is an ethical responsibility to be open to the other, and it is an ethical responsibility to maintain a degree of security in the process—if not for ourselves, then for others for whom we are responsible, including those others to whom we have already offered hospitality. We cannot simply choose hospitality and forego security. Yet I believe that the meanest and most shameful moments in American religious history have been borne of an inclination toward security. And that the most just and humane moments have been borne of an idealistic, indeed risky inclination toward hospitality.

Although I can't pretend to offer a political solution in this little book, I do hope to encourage a hard lean toward hospitality, even at some greater risk to security, not only in the realm of law and policy but also in local neighborhoods and homes, and also in hearts and minds.

Chapter 1

Local Landscapes

Exploring the Neighborhood

Religion is always first and foremost local; it lives and thrives in particular places, cultures, and people. Is there even such a thing as religion in general? Yet we do love generalizing about it. We love making broad, sweeping statements about religious people we don't know, about different religions, and about religion in general. When we do, we're likely to reveal little about anything religious and a lot about ourselves, especially our foolish tendency to simplify everything and everyone but ourselves.

In an exploration as very short and very broad as ours, then, we'll be wise to keep in mind those local, particular, sometimes peculiar manifestations of religion in America that we encounter in the course of our daily lives at school, at home, and at work—as well as in the course of our commuting *between* those places. For it is often in traversing such in-between spaces that we come into brief, passing contact with some of the wide variety of religious groups and institutions with which we do not identify. Taking these in, we begin to catch a glimpse of the stunning diversity and dynamic complexity of religion in America today. So let me begin with two local religious landscapes: my own daily five-mile, ten-minute commute to and from work at my university; and my own university campus community.

Commute

Like most people, I'm usually too busy thinking about what n[...]
to happen when I get to work to pay much mind to what I'm
passing at twenty-five miles per hour, or so, on my way there. No[...]
that I've begun to pay more attention, however, I'm gaining a
whole new sense of relationship and connection to the local
neighborhoods through which I travel each day. The reality of my
surroundings has changed, and my understanding of the rich
diversity of religion in America has become more intimate.

I live in an old house on the western end of Shaker Heights, a small
inner-ring suburban city that butts up against the city of Cleveland.
Purported to be the first planned suburb in the United States, this
small city began more than a century ago as a white Protestant
utopian community built by the venture capitalist Van Swearingen
brothers on land purchased from the dwindling North Union
settlement of Shakers, who lived there from 1822 to 1889.

The lives of those settlers trace their way into the present in the
form of old gateposts, grindstones, dams, and a boulder with a
small plaque that marks a mass grave of bodies moved from a
Shaker graveyard in 1909 to make way for urban development.
Their religious culture is remembered annually, if oddly, in the
elementary schools on "Shaker Day," when kids don bonnets and/
or overalls, enjoy Shaker-style lemon pie, and sing the well-known
Shaker hymn, "'Tis the Gift to Be Simple."

Shaker simplicity notwithstanding, in 1962 Shaker Heights
boasted the highest per capita income in the United States. For
decades, moreover, the city intentionally excluded African
Americans and Jews (as well as most Roman Catholics). Since the
1970s it has proactively promoted racial integration and cultural
pluralism, facing its own and the larger American heritages of
racism and ethnocentrism directly and honestly. And although it

a self-consciously Protestant community, today it sees as
ewish bat mitzvahs and bar mitzvahs and Catholic first
nunions as Protestant confirmations on any given weekend,
it is happy to welcome growing numbers of Hindu and Muslim
esidents among many others.

As I back down my driveway I see the tall white steeple of Plymouth
Church, which is part of the United Church of Christ denomination.
This massive brick church with four large pillars in front was built
in 1916 to be "the Community Church" of Shaker Heights. Now the
home of a progressive, liberal congregation, its steeple bells still
play traditional Protestant Christian hymns at midday, awakening
nostalgic joy or Christian devotion in some residents, and feelings
of resentment or bewilderment in others.

Just behind Plymouth Church is Shaker Square, home of the North
Union Farmers Market. On Saturday mornings, Amish women in
starched light blue dresses come there with their bearded husbands
to sell wholesome goods. Most residents know far less about their
religious beliefs and practices than they do about their superb
vegetables, homemade pies and jams, and handmade rugs and
furniture.

Turning onto the gently curving, mansion-lined boulevard that
divides Shaker Heights from the neighboring city of Cleveland
Heights, I enter an intersection whose four corners are each
occupied by major religious institutions. On one corner is the
familiar high rock wall of Beaumont Convent, whose Ursuline nuns
run the attached Beaumont School for girls. The oldest secondary
school in the Cleveland area, it was started by the Ursuline Sisters
and a laywoman from France in 1850. In 1942 the Sisters moved the
school to its present location on a twenty-seven-acre estate.

Across the street from the Beaumont Convent and School is yet
another vestige of Cleveland's cloistered history, the monastery of
the Cleveland Carmelite Sisters, established in 1923. The Order of

Carmel goes back to the hermits who settled on Mount Carmel the Holy Land during the Christian Crusades. Soul sisters to the biblical prophet Elijah, who encountered God while alone on Mount Carmel, the Carmelite Sisters today are devoted to prayerful solitude.

On another corner of the same intersection is True Sisters Child Care Center, a day care and preschool that has been maintained since 1945 by the Order of True Sisters, a Jewish women's service organization that began in New York in 1846 as a secret society devoted to the principles of faith and love.

And on the fourth corner of that intersection is the massive First Church of Christ, Scientist, built in 1930 in the Beaux Arts architectural style. Its members meet on Sunday mornings and Wednesday evenings to share testimonials of healing and religious insight, and to read and study their scriptures (the Bible and *Science and Health with Key to the Scriptures*, written by the Mother Church's founder, Mary Baker Eddy). Not far from here is a century-old hotel, the Alcazar, which now serves as a Christian Science retirement home.

Down the boulevard half a mile, at the next lighted intersection, are two more "big steeple" churches, both with reputations as mainstays of liberal-intellectual, high-culture Christianity. On one corner is the sandstone tower of Fairmount Presbyterian Church. Now one of the largest Presbyterian churches in the area with 1,300 members, it began in 1915 as a small frame chapel for Sunday school classes. Two years later that building was struck by lightning and burned to the ground. Apparently refusing to take that as a sign from God, the congregation continued to meet. Today, it takes pride in its reputation for outstanding preaching and its commitment, since the 1960s, to racial integration.

On the other side of the street, rivaling Fairmount's sandstone tower, is the 125-foot tower of Saint Paul's Episcopal Church, home

...ce the 1920s of the oldest Episcopal congregation in the ...leveland area (first established downtown in 1846), which now numbers well over 2,000 members. With a long-standing reputation for educational programming, Saint Paul's is also the home of the Cleveland Ecumenical Institute for Religious Studies, which offers college-level courses on religion to lay people of all religious and nonreligious perspectives and backgrounds.

Both Fairmount and Saint Paul's, moreover, are members of the Interfaith Hospitality Network, which works with dozens of congregations from many different religious traditions to provide homeless families with temporary housing, personal and professional counseling, and related services.

A minute later I'm winding my way down Fairmount Boulevard toward University Circle, a one-square-mile area surrounding Case Western Reserve University that includes more than thirty educational, cultural, and healthcare centers. Among these are a variety of religious institutions: the inconspicuous old colonial Quaker meetinghouse of the Cleveland Society of Friends and its neighbor, the Latter-day Saints Church Institute (the university's School of Dentistry has a large number of Mormon students); the conspicuously proud cathedralesque buildings of the Pentecostal Church of Christ, the Epworth United Methodist Church (affectionately known as "the oil can church" for its massive copper roof and spire), and the vast, Byzantine-style limestone Temple Tifereth Israel, often called "Silver's Temple" after Rabbi Hillel Silver, who served as rabbi from 1917 to 1963. Silver was a national leader of Reform Judaism and a major voice in the United Nations' establishment of the state of Israel.

In the center of the university campus is the Church of the Covenant, a Presbyterian church boasting an outstanding organ, a heritage of great preaching, a commitment to promoting interreligious dialogue, and a passion for social justice. Most recently it has become home to the Northeast Ohio Alliance for

1. Temple Tifereth Israel, a Reform Jewish temple in University Circle, Cleveland. It is affectionately known as Silver's Temple, after Abba Hillel Silver, who served as its rabbi from 1917 to 1963.

Hope, an interreligious organization focused on working with businesses and policy makers to address systemic forms of racism and poverty in Cleveland.

On the outskirts of University Circle, where new construction is still possible, we find more recent religious arrivals. On the south edge of campus is the small, windowless, wood frame building of the India Community Center. Built in 1978, it merged with the Indian student association at the university in 1980 to become the Federation of India Community Associations for the Cleveland area.

After work, an alternate route home takes me through Cleveland's neighborhoods of Fairfax, Woodland Hills, and Buckeye-Shaker, which butts up against Shaker Heights's west end. Known in the early 1900s as "Little Hungary" on account of their large immigrant populations, today these neighborhoods are

...inantly African American. Decades ago, they were home to ...ng communities, but they have suffered tremendously in ...e recent years from the decline of Cleveland's industrial ...onomy, the loss of school funding, and white flight to the ...uburbs. Today, more than 40 percent of the populations in these neighborhoods live below the poverty line. Still, with assistance from the city, sweat equity from the interreligious organization Habitat for Humanity, and active commitment from several local churches and religious groups, these neighborhoods are rallying to new revitalization initiatives that draw creatively from their rich local histories for inspiration.

As I drive out of University Circle along Cedar Avenue, I can see the modern white tower and blue dome of the Uqbah Mosque Foundation on the next block. This mosque was established and built by the university's Muslim Student Association. It now serves not only students but also many Muslim families in the area. Its president, who also directs the MSA on campus, has been heavily involved, especially since 2001, in promoting a deeper understanding and appreciation of Islam among non-Muslims.

Farther down the avenue, beyond the old, white wooden chapel of Calvary Hill Baptist Church, I come to a major focal point of African American urban activism and community building, Antioch Baptist Church, which has been a leader in community economic development and AIDS prevention in Cleveland. Its minister, the Reverend Dr. Marvin A. McMickle, is a nationally known preacher, author, and longtime advocate of civil rights in the city.

Directly across the street from Antioch Baptist is a more recent arrival to the city's African American religious scene, the United House of Prayer for All People. Like this holiness movement's mother church in Atlanta, Georgia, known as "Love's Corner" and led by the Honorable S. C. (Sweet Daddy) Madison, this church's grandiose, brown brick building and steep, glimmering golden aluminum roof are far from any traditional "churchy" look. Giant lion sculptures stand on either side of a broad stairway leading to the sanctuary. Jubilant angels reach toward the heavens from twin towers decorated with spiraling stripes like brick candy sticks. A bold mix of spiritual exuberance and whimsy.

Turning south from Cedar on East Seventy-ninth Street, I pass several more churches, including Saint James African Methodist Episcopal Church, Faith Tabernacle, Second Baptist Church Metropolitan, Emmanuel Baptist Church, and the Original Church of God, which stands directly across the street from the closed and boarded Langston Hughes Center (Hughes lived in this area for several years as a child). Across from a used tire shop is an old single-story warehouse building that's been converted, with a lot of white paint and some simple signage, into In the Way Missionary Baptist Church.

I take a left on Woodland and head up the short hill for a few blocks toward my hometown of Shaker Heights. In this short distance I see a few more large churches, but what captures my attention and imagination are all the tiny "storefront churches"—nine by my count: the Church of God and Saints of Christ, First Tabernacle; New Revelation Baptist Church; Faith Holiness Temple; Kingdom Life Assembly Church; Faith Pentecostal Church of Jesus Christ; Dawson Temple Church of God in Christ; Greater Fellowship Assembly; Pentecostal Faith Holiness Church of God; and the Harvard Apostolic Overcoming Holy Church of God. Standing between abandoned houses and piles of rubbish from buildings that have been demolished as part of the Buckeye area redevelopment plan, these little makeshift chapels have no spires, no bell towers, no stained glass. No glass at all, in fact. On the solid walls where you'd expect to see windows are paintings of windows. While the threat of break-ins prevents the use of real windows, the members of these little churches understand, nonetheless, that windows express hospitality and openness to the outside.

> City people have acted on and with the spaces of the city to make religious meanings in many different ways. They have appropriated public spaces for themselves and transformed them into venues for shaping, displaying, and celebrating their inherited and emergent ways of life and understandings of the world. They have remapped the city, superimposing their own coordinates of meaning on official cartographies ... creating a distinctly urban palimpsest.
>
> —Robert A. Orsi, *Gods of the City*

Each storefront church bears simple signage that, like the painted-on windows, reveals much and little about the lives of their leaders and congregations. The Church of God and Saints of Christ, First Tabernacle, a tiny, brown brick box at the bottom of the hill, holds services on the actual Sabbath, that is, Friday evening and Saturday, and calls its pastor "Rabbi."

A sign on the wood framed house of Faith Pentecostal Church of Jesus Christ indicates that its pastor, Lula B. Ford, is also its founder. Just above its painted-on window are the words, "MOMA IF YOU LOVE ME TAKE ME TO CHURCH."

Painted in bold capital letters on Dawson Temple are the words "PEACE-LOVE-JOY" with an arrow pointing at the front door. To the right are two annexes: a day-care center, and Dawson Temple Carry Out offering "chicken, fish, Polish Boys, etc."

A little way up the road, near a high school, among a string of old houses turned antique shops and thrift stores, is the home of the Interdenominational Church Ushers Association, part of a national African American organization with more than 30,000 members dedicated to strengthening and supporting those who serve as church ushers, welcoming guests and strangers to worship services. The organization was established in 1919 to help break

2. Lula B. Ford's Faith Pentecostal Church of Jesus Christ in the Woodland neighborhood of Cleveland. Above its painted-on window: "MOMA IF YOU LOVE ME TAKE ME TO CHURCH."

down barriers of discrimination and prejudice that kept churches from welcoming guests of different racial or class backgrounds.

The many religious institutions and organizations that I've described so far are only those parts of the religious landscape that have frontage on the streets I drive during my short commute. Not far out of view from my car window are dozens of others—synagogues, yeshivas, Catholic churches, Protestant churches, storefront churches, a Hungarian Roman Catholic church, a Unity church, a Unitarian Universalist church, a yoga center, and the "City Buddha" store, to name a few.

And that's only the obvious stuff, with property, and buildings, and signs. Who knows how many mezuzahs containing small Hebrew scrolls of the Shema ("Hear, O Israel, . . . ") are affixed to doorposts; how many Ganeshas, Shivas, Blessed Virgin Marys, and Buddhas stand in kitchen windows and on tables in homemade meditation rooms; how many scriptures of how many different religious traditions lay open on bed stands and desks and mantles; how many groups are gathered in houses for Shabbat dinners, hymn sings, Bible studies, Santería ceremonies, Jain weddings; how many people sit in front of monitors exploring religion on the Internet, or IMing one another with ultimate questions about spirituality.

Campus

Such is the religious landscape of my commute to and from school. What about the university campus itself?

Although my university is steadfastly secular, it has deep historical roots in Protestant Christian tradition. Like so many institutions and cultural environments in contemporary America, it would be most aptly described as post-religious. The women's college and the men's college that came together to form Western Reserve College were both Protestant schools with clearly Christian educational missions. Vestiges of this heritage remain everywhere: biblical verses inscribed on exterior walls of old dormitory buildings; the tree of the knowledge of good and evil and the tree of life carved into a stone arch at the old entrance to the women's college; and, most visibly, two large stone chapels. Once places of regular worship and prayer for students, faculty, and staff, they now host musical performances, lectures, and academic ceremonies, as well as occasional weddings of couples that may lack church membership but still want—and are willing to pay for—the nostalgia of a classic American chapel wedding.

To say that the university as an institution is post-religious is not to say that its student body or larger community is. In fact, like most research universities today—especially those, like this one, with large numbers of international students and first- and second-generation immigrants from East and South Asia—the student body is far more religiously vibrant and diverse than ever before.

Although there has been a general awareness of the significance of religion and religious diversity on campus, no one had a clear sense of how significant religion on campus is until a few years ago, when students in my senior seminar in religious studies began conducting research on the subject. Inspired by Harvard's Pluralism Project, which focuses primarily on research and education on religious diversity, we called our seminar the Case Pluralism Project.

Our main goals were to map the religious landscape of our roughly 4,000 undergraduate students as comprehensively and complexly as possible, and to gain a fuller understanding of the variety of ways that religion impacts undergraduate education and life. Working in small groups, the students focused their research on three distinct yet interrelated dimensions of religion on campus: the curricular dimension (study and discussion of religion in the classroom, in the sciences as well as in the humanities); the extracurricular dimension (religious organizations, the impact of religion on social interactions outside the classroom, etc.); and the personal dimension (the importance of religion in the personal lives of students). We conducted interviews with students, faculty members, leaders of religious organizations, and staff members in the offices of student life; we observed meetings and events hosted by student religious organizations; and we conducted a survey of more than 600 undergraduate students, representing every class and field of study.

More than 70 percent of the undergraduate students at this secular research university identify with one or more religious traditions (more than 80 percent say that their parents do), and the majority of them name some form of Protestant or Catholic Christianity (25.8 percent and 24.3 percent, respectively). Yet there were significant numbers representing other religious identities: 5.8 percent Jewish; 3.8 percent Hindu; 3.1 percent Muslim; 2 percent Buddhist; 1.3 percent Orthodox Christian (Coptic, Greek, Ukrainian, etc.); 3.3 percent other religious traditions, including Baha'i, Jain, Jehovah's Witness, Unitarian, and Satanism. Interestingly, about 5 percent of students identify themselves with two or more religious traditions. Some of these hybrid religious identities include Buddhist/Christian, Buddhist/Jewish, Jewish/Christian, Jewish/Atheist, and Jain/Christian. There is every reason to expect that all these smaller percentages, including the hybrids, will continue to grow in the years and decades to come.

About one-third of the students are involved in student religious organizations, and many of those organizations are more vocal and interactive with one another than ever before, thanks especially to the new Interfaith Center. Located in the east wing of the Church of the Covenant, it is headquarters for three campus religious organizations, the United Protestant Campus Ministries, Newman Catholic Campus Ministry, and the Muslim Student Association. The center works closely with the Hillel Jewish Student Center in a neighboring building, and with campus organizations for Baha'i, Hindu, and Buddhist students, among others. The Interfaith Center has a shared space for various religious services. Catholic students celebrate Mass in their socks so that the same space can serve as the prayer room for Muslims, who prostrate themselves toward Mecca five times a day.

It's commonplace to hear that students become less religious in the course of their college years. Yet our research suggests otherwise. One of the questions we asked was, "How would you describe yourself? Religious, spiritual, both, or neither?" Although fewer

Case Pluralism Project
How would you describe yourself?

	Religious	Spiritual	Both	Neither
Freshmen	18%	29%	25%	25%
Sophomores	17%	28%	28%	25%
Juniors	19%	27%	27%	24%
Seniors	10%	33%	35%	22%

Case Pluralism Project survey data. Here, the 635 student responses are correlated to class standing. Although fewer seniors than first-year students describe themselves as "religious," more of them describe themselves as "spiritual" or "both" religious and spiritual. Note, too, that slightly fewer seniors than first-years describe themselves as "neither" religious nor spiritual. Percentages are rounded to the nearest whole number.

seniors (about 10 percent) than first-year students (18 percent) describe themselves as "religious," more of them describe themselves as "spiritual" or "both" religious and spiritual (33 and 35 percent) than do first-year students (29 percent and 25 percent). Moreover, the number of seniors who describe themselves as "neither" religious nor spiritual is actually a few percent *lower* than the number of first-year students who do.

Religion on our campus is gendered in many significant respects. Considerably more men than women describe themselves as "neither" religious nor spiritual (about 31 percent of them, whereas only 18 percent of women do). Not that men are less vocal about religion, however. Whereas more than half of men say that they are comfortable sharing their views about religion in class, only about a third of women say they are. At the same time, most student religious organizations and clubs are led by women.

Cautions

I share the religious landscapes of my daily commute and my campus community because, in many respects, I see them as microcosms of religion in America: rich in historical complexity; still predominantly Christian, but diversely so; growing ever more religiously plural every year, as new cultural groups from around the world make their homes here, and as new religious movements and hybrid religious identities emerge in what is anything but a melting pot; in a constant state of change reflecting larger social transformations brought on by a range of forces, including, to name a few, the information revolution, globalization, and consumerism; changing social dynamics within religious communities, often involving increased opportunities for leadership by women. Like Horton's Who-ville, what we often discover in our own neighborhoods are miniature copies of the landscape of religion in America as a whole.

In another sense, however, my local religious landscapes are utterly unique, worlds unto themselves, radically different from yours, whatever those may be. In fact, every local landscape has its own particularly complex patchwork of religiosity, which reflects its own peculiar inhabitants and unique histories of immigration and emigration, settling and unsettling, economic welfare and disparity, and so on.

I often remind my students that the study of religion, like most research in the humanities and social sciences, is rich in paradoxes. For religious people, for example, the sacred is revealed in the profane, which is by definition its opposite; self comes into contact with otherness, and one discovers the other in oneself. Similarly, for students of religious studies, coming to an understanding of an unfamiliar religious worldview or experience involves the strange becoming familiar, and the familiar becoming strange; the other is discovered in oneself, and vice versa.

Here's another paradox: the closer you look, the more you see. Most of us think we can see more from a wide-angle view, by gaining some distance and perspective and taking in the whole landscape. But what we learn when we zoom in and get close to our subjects is that there are stunningly diverse and complex worlds within the tiniest patches of society, and that these tiny worlds are interconnected with the worlds around them in innumerable and subtly complex ways. Our social, cultural, and personal realities unfold downward toward greater and greater complexity and diversity. In a very real sense, there's no getting to the bottom of things. The farther down you go, the more you see.

This is a paradox that can only be discovered through experience. In *Pilgrim at Tinker Creek*, Annie Dillard discovered it along the edges of the stream behind her house. When discussing her beautiful essay, "On Seeing," with my students, I ask them each to go outside, find a six-inch patch of ground, and see what she or he can see in a half hour or so. It can be a revelatory experience. They often return with extensive reports that go into great detail about little worlds rich unto themselves and at the same time closely connected with everything around them. So it is with the tiny patchworks of America's religious landscape.

That has certainly been my experience in my own religious backyard. I had no idea how much I'd find, and I still have no idea how much more there is. I've barely scratched the surface. Certainly there's enough behind the painted-on front window of any one of those storefront churches to fill a fat book (*Pilgrim at Dawson Temple* . . .). There's part of me that thinks that that would be a better approach to writing a book about religion in America than the one I'm taking.

As we proceed to the next chapter to get the "big picture" view of the religious landscape of the nation as a whole, let's keep two cautions in mind.

First, we must take care to avoid gross generalizations about religion in America. Certainly such hubris is common these days among scholars and journalists, especially among the cultured among its despisers, and a lot of people are paying attention to them. We should remember, nonetheless, that behind every sweeping description and statistic are very particular local persons and groups whose stories are in many ways absolutely unique, even when they have much in common with others.

Second, we must avoid thinking of "religion in America" in static terms. The one constant here is change. Snapshots and profiles can mislead us by suggesting more permanence and stability than actually exist. Religious beliefs, practices, and institutions are always changing, despite how their own adherents and leaders often represent them. The same goes for particular religious individuals and communities within any religious tradition.

Chapter 2

The Big Picture

Religion in America by the Numbers, and Then Some

Here, let's try to get a satellite's-eye view of religion in America today. How many people in America are Christian? How many are Jewish? Muslim, Buddhist, Hindu? Rastafarian, Wiccan, Druid? Atheist? Are there concentrations of particular religious groups in different regions of the United States? Which numbers are growing? Which are shrinking?

It is tempting these days to think that all we need to know is religion in America by the numbers. We live under a statistical dictatorship, a tyranny of numbers. Billions of dollars annually are invested in counting. Market research, surveys, polls, educational testing, outcomes assessment.... It seems that anything worth our attention can be quantified.

But counting is only one way to measure religious diversity and the felt presence of particular religions in America. In fact, numbers can be misleading. As I mentioned in chapter 1, the total number of Jewish, Muslim, and Baha'i students on my college campus is relatively low. But one would be profoundly mistaken to equate the relative numeric insignificance of these three student populations with insignificant social presence on campus. All three groups have very active, influential student organizations on campus. Especially since 9/11, the Muslim Student Association has done a great deal to educate other students about Islam, in all *its* diversity, through participation in interreligious panels and through inviting non-Muslims to attend special celebrations, especially during Ramadan. Likewise the Hillel group, which invites non-Jewish students to attend Passover seders and Sukkot festivals on campus. And the Baha'i student organization has provided campus leadership in initiatives to promote nonviolence and struggle against racism.

As we map the religious diversity of America today, we'll surely want to look at the numbers, drawing from various surveys and polls taken by national organizations and by specific religious groups. But we'll also want to pay attention to those presences on the American religious landscape that barely register numerically, for they nonetheless reveal a great deal about religion in America today, and tomorrow. Here I refer especially to those new religious movements, or NRMs, that dot our map (with more dots every year), as well as growing numbers of individuals and groups whose religious identities involve hybrid combinations of elements from different, sometimes even historically oppositional or antithetical, religious traditions. And we'll also want to consider the powerful influence of religion in the public spheres of popular culture and politics, most notably the rise of the Religious Right, an ecumenical movement with a strong evangelical Christian core.

By the numbers

One of the greatest challenges to determining the religious diversity of America by the numbers is finding reliable, widely agreed-upon population statistics. The U. S. Census does not include religious identity in its accounting of the population. Some religious groups keep very close counts of assemblies (churches, synagogues, meditation centers) and members. Many others do not. Those that do, moreover, often have very different definitions of membership.

Any research on religious diversity in America must necessarily base itself on a particular definition of religious identity. Must a person exhibit certain signs of commitment to a religious group based on regular attendance? Do I have to attend a Presbyterian church to be Presbyterian? How many times per year? Or must a person perform certain ritual practices? Am I Catholic if I don't take Holy Communion regularly or if I'm not baptized? Am I Jewish if I didn't have a bar mitzvah? Or must one profess specific doctrines or beliefs? Am I a Baptist if I don't believe what the Nicene Creed says about the Trinity or resurrection of the body? Given the major differences between different religious traditions (e.g., concerning the premiums placed on belief or "faith" versus practice), we should wonder whether it is even possible to establish a single set of criteria for religious identity that works for all religions.

Because there is no universal or even widely accepted objective standard for religious identity, the best research focuses on the *subjective* standard of self-identification. The fullest and most reliable recent study that takes this approach is the 2001 American Religious Identification Survey (ARIS), based on a survey of more than 50,000 Americans, by Barry A. Kosmin, Egon Mayer, and Ariela Keysar of the Graduate Center of the City University of New York. ARIS is a follow-up study from the National Survey of Religious Identification (NSRI) conducted in 1990, and both were designed to compensate for the lack of religious data in the U. S. Census (conducted in 1990 and 2000).

Another important source for our data on religious identity in America is the *Yearbook of American and Canadian Churches*, an annual report on membership and other details (financial, governmental structure) for all Christian groups as well as for many other religious organizations, published by the National Council of Churches in the U.S. and edited by Eileen W. Linder. Both sets of data allow us to see not only the current numbers but also trends of growth and decline. The information presented here

Self Described Religious Identification of U.S. Adult Population, 1990–2001

(Weighted Estimate)

TOTAL U.S. ADULT POPULATION 18+

1990 = 175,440,000   2001 = 207,980,000

Christian Religious Groups	1990 Number	%	2001 Number	%
Catholic	46,004,000		50,873,000	24.5
Baptist	33,964,000		33,830,000	16.3
Protestant - no denomination supplied	17,214,000		4,647,000	2.2
Methodist/Wesleyan	14,174,000		14,150,000	6.8
Lutheran	9,110,000		9,580,000	4.6
Christian - no denomination supplied	8,073,000		14,190,000	6.8
Presbyterian	4,985,000		5,596,000	2.7
Pentecostal/Charismatic	3,191,000		4,407,000	2.1
Episcopalian/Anglican	3,042,000		3,451,000	1.7
Mormon/Latter-Day Saints	2,487,000		2,787,000	1.3
Churches of Christ	1,769,000		2,503,000	1.2
Jehovah's Witness	1,381,000		1,331,000	0.6
Seventh-Day Adventist	668,000		724,000	0.3
Assemblies of God	660,000		1,106,000	0.5
Holiness/Holy	610,000		569,000	0.3
Congregational/United Church of Christ	599,000		1,378,000	0.7
Church of the Nazarene	549,000		544,000	0.3
Church of God	531,000		944,000	0.5
Orthodox (Eastern)	502,000		645,000	
Evangelical	242,000		1,032,000	0.5
Mennonite	235,000		346,000	
Christian Science	214,000		194,000	
Church of the Brethren	206,000		358,000	
Born Again	204,000		56,000	
Nondenominational	195,000		2,489,000	1.2
Disciples of Christ	144,000		492,000	
Reformed/Dutch Reform	161,000		289,000	
Apostolic/New Apostolic	117,000		254,000	
Quaker	67,000		217,000	
Full Gospel	51,000		168,000	
Christian Reform	40,000		79,000	
Foursquare Gospel	28,000		70,000	
Fundamentalist	27,000		61,000	
Salvation Army	27,000		25,000	
Independent Christian Church	25,000		71,000	
TOTAL Christian	**151,225,00**	**86.2**	**159,030,000**	**76.5**

Other Religion Groups	1990		2001	
	Number	%	Number	%
Jewish	3,137,000		2,831,000	1.3
Muslim/Islamic	527,000		1,104,000	0.5
Buddhist	401,000		1,082,000	0.5
Unitarian/Universalist	502,000		629,000	0.3
Hindu	227,000		766,000	0.4
Native American	47,000		103,000	
Scientologist	45,000		55,000	
Baha'I	28,000		84,000	
Taoist	23,000		40,000	
New Age	20,000		68,000	
Eckankar	18,000		26,000	
Rastafarian	14,000		11,000	
Sikh	13,000		57,000	
Wiccan	8,000		134,000	
Deity	6,000		49,000	
Druid			33,000	
Santeria			22,000	
Pagan			140,000	
Spiritualist			116,000	
Ethical Culture			4,000	
Other unclassified	837,000		386,000	
Total Other Religions	**5,853,000**	**3.3**	**7,740,000**	**3.7**

No Religion Groups	1990		2001	
	Number	%	Number	%
Atheist			902,000	0.4
Agnostic	1186000		991,000	0.5
Humanist	29,000		49,000	0
Secular			53,000	0
No Religion	13,116,000		27,486,000	13.2
Total No Religion Specified	**14,331,000**	**8.2**	**29,481,000**	**14.1**
Refused	**4,031,000**	**2.3**	**11,246,000**	**5.4**

"What is your religion, if any?" Self-Described Religious Identification of U.S. Adult Population—1990 and 2001. American Religious Identification Survey. Source: Figure 2.1 from Barry A. Kosmin and Ariela Keysar, *Religion in a Free Market: Religious and Non-Religious Americans, Who, What, Why, Where* (Paramount Market Publishing, Inc., 2006). Weighted estimates based on 2001 survey of more than 50,000 subjects.

draws primarily from ARIS, using the *Yearbook* for supplemental details on particular religious groups.

On first impression, the numbers offer no big surprises. The vast majority of Americans (over 80 percent) identify themselves as religious, and the vast majority of those (95 percent) identify with some form of Christianity. About one-third of Christians are Catholic and about two-thirds (about half of the U.S. population) identify with some form of Protestantism.

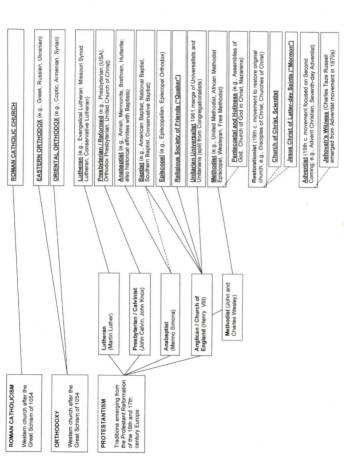

Simplified family tree of Christian traditions in America. Boxes on the right side represent the main family groups present in the United States today. Although the denominations listed as examples in each group have common historical roots, their theologies and practices are often very different (e.g., American Baptists versus Southern Baptists, or Disciples of Christ versus Churches of Christ). *Hannah Whitehead and Timothy Beal*

According to the *Yearbook*, the three fastest growing Christian groups are Catholic, Assemblies of God, and the Church of Jesus Christ of Latter-day Saints (Mormonism). The three that have experienced the highest rate of decline are the Presbyterian Church (USA), American Baptist Churches, and the Evangelical Lutheran Church (all theologically liberal Christian denominations). Six of the fifteen largest churches in the United States are predominantly African American.

The total of all Americans that identify with other religious traditions (Judaism, Islam, Buddhism, Hinduism, and so on) adds up to less than 4 percent of the population. Among these, Judaism is by far the largest population, representing 1.3 percent of Americans. Other survey data claim higher numbers for Judaism but do not distinguish self-identification with Judaism as a religion, as ARIS does.

But look a little more closely and the American religious landscape begins to appear far less homogeneous and unchanging. First, note that there are thirty-six different categories of Christianity listed here (including Unitarian Universalism, which ARIS includes in "Other Religions"), representing a very wide range of traditions. Note too that there were many others named by subjects, but they were lumped together into these larger subcategories. Although all of them have their historical roots in Christian theology and tradition, and although most would identify themselves as Christian, many would not identify others within the larger category as Christian. Most Baptists and Fundamentalists, for example, would not acknowledge Mormonism or Christian Science as Christian.

In fact, the nearly 77 percent of Americans who self-identify as Christian are a diverse *pluribus* of *Christianities* that are far from any collective unity.

Remember, moreover, that this data is based on *self-identification*. American culture remains predominantly Christian-oriented in many respects, at least superficially. We may well suspect, therefore, that a higher percentage of those who identify themselves as Christian (esp. "Christian—no denomination supplied" and "Protestant—no denomination supplied") do so simply because it is culturally normative to do so.

Although the number of Americans who identify with religions other than Christianity is still a fairly low percentage of the total population, moreover, many of these religious populations are growing rapidly. The fastest growing religion is Wicca, closely followed by Paganism, although both are still very small in total numbers. The Jewish population decreased slightly between 1990 and 2001 (from 3.1 million to 2.8 million; other data sources give higher numbers but nonetheless show an overall decline), but the number of Muslims more than doubled, from 500,000 to 1.1 million. So did the number of Americans who identify with Buddhism, Hinduism, Sikhism, or Taoism—from 1.1 million to 2.6 million in all. Recent research by the Pluralism Project and other groups suggests that these numbers have continued to grow rapidly since 2001.

Much of this historically unprecedented growth is due to changes in patterns of American immigration, especially since the Immigration and Nationality Act of 1965, which opened the doors to more newcomers from Asia representing religious traditions such as Buddhism, Hinduism, Islam, and Jainism, among others (see chapter 5).

But immigration is not the whole story. In fact, some of the growth among minority religious groups in America is due to conversion. According to ARIS, about 16 percent of adults in America have changed religious identities. Among the religions with "net gains" on account of "switching in" are Buddhism and Islam (12 and 8 percent, respectively).

Note too that the total number of Christian Americans has dropped substantially since 1990—from more than 86 percent to under 77 percent. Closely related is the sharp increase in the number of Americans who do not identify with any religion. In fact, the number of Americans who are secular grew by about 60 percent between 1990 and 2001—from 14.3 million (8.2 percent) to 29.4 million (14.1 percent).

No doubt the emergence of a critical mass of secularists is one of the reasons why we are seeing religion put on the cultural front burner of public discourse in new ways these days. Most notable here are the huge American markets for sweeping attacks on religion, especially Christianity, by best-selling authors such as Richard Dawkins, Sam Harris, and Christopher Hitchens. Ironically, many of the generalizations about religion lobbed by these nonreligious critics are as intellectually irresponsible as the polemical attacks common *between* religious groups. Religious diversity, including a growing number of nonreligious people, is on the rise. Religious literacy, not so much.

Gender, age, and ethnicity are significant factors with regard to religious identity and *nonreligious* identity. As was the case in our student survey, discussed in the previous chapter, women are more likely than men to describe themselves as religious (42 percent versus 31 percent) and less likely to describe themselves as secular (8 percent versus 12 percent); older people are more likely than younger people to describe themselves as religious; African Americans are least likely to describe themselves as secular, whereas Asian Americans are most likely to do so.

Region is also an important variable in both religious and nonreligious identity. According to ARIS, the highest percentages of nonreligious people are in the West (so-called left coast), averaging around 20 percent. The southern states lean strongly toward Baptist tradition. Utah is 54 percent Mormon. Rhode Island is more than half Catholic (51 percent). At 5 percent, New York has the largest Jewish religious population (4 percent in New Jersey; 3 percent in both Florida and Maryland).

Religious identity and political orientation sometimes coincide, but not always. As we might expect, the majority of evangelical Christians (58 percent) and Mormons (55 percent) are Republican, whereas only a small number of them are Democrat (12 percent and 14 percent respectively; the rest are Independent or nonidentified). Only nine percent of Buddhists are Republican, 31 percent are Democrat, and 48 percent are Independent (the other 12 percent are nonidentified). Jewish religious people are mostly Democrat (56 percent), with relatively few Republicans (13 percent). Within Islam, Democrats outnumber Republicans by twofold (35 percent to 19 percent), but the highest numbers (39 percent) are Independent. Some might be surprised to find that there are almost as many Democrats (33 percent) as there are Republicans (39 percent) among Baptists, and that there are considerably more Republicans (46 percent) than Democrats (25 percent) among Presbyterians. Overall, the political orientations of religious Americans are fairly evenly spread, with about 30 percent in each of the main affiliations (Democrat, Republican, and Independent), and the remaining one-tenth identifying with another political party (Green, Libertarian, Communist) or none at all.

Religious *identity* and religious *practice* do not necessarily go together. Many people who call themselves religious are not actually affiliated with religious groups. Although 80 percent of Americans identify themselves as religious, only 54 percent belong to a religious organization, such as a mosque, a synagogue, or a church. According to the great scholar of religion Émile Durkheim, religion is fundamentally social, a unified system of beliefs and practices that are concerned essentially with creating social unity and coherence. For many Americans today, however, being religious is entirely personal and has no necessary relation to participation in a larger religious community. Perhaps Durkheim would say that they are therefore not religious. Many religious people in other parts of the world would agree. These Americans apparently would not.

Many would also presume that religious identity is singular and total, demanding one's whole self in commitment to an exclusive, all-encompassing worldview. Limit: one religion per person. In the campus survey that we conducted, we asked students if they identified with "one or more religious traditions," and then left room for as many as they wished to name. A significant percentage of students (about 5 percent) indicated more than one religious identity. Most research polls (including ARIS) do not allow for such hybrid religious identities.

Would the population of religious hybrids be as high for the general American population? Probably not. Not yet, anyway. In our survey, there was a high correlation between students who identified with two or more religions and those whose two parents identified with different religious traditions. According to ARIS, 22 percent of all households with married or domestic partners involved mixed religious identities (the highest numbers being among Buddhists and Episcopalians; the lowest being among Mormons, Baptists, and other conservative Christian denominations). Many of those adults do not personally identify with both religious traditions, but many of their children do. In the general population, including all ages, the number of people with hybrid religious identities would probably not be as high as they are among the young adults in our study. Still, as we'll discuss in chapter 5, it is likely that the number of hybrid, even "build-your-own" religious identities will grow in the coming years.

The generalization that the American religious landscape remains predominantly Christian can be misleading. Even a quick look at the numbers over ten years' time indicates that the reality is far more complex and dynamic. Religious diversity is a reality, and its felt presence in American society is growing daily. It includes a very diverse range of Christianities that are often in disagreement with one another over key issues of doctrine and practice, and with those rapidly growing populations of many other religions. And it includes a growing number of Americans who are not religious at

l. <u>Religious diversity in America</u> today is greater than it has ever been in recorded human history.

And again, there's more to the picture than what the numbers can show. Some of the most fascinating aspects of our landscape are not easily quantified. To get the fullest possible picture of religion in America today, we need to attend to them. Here, then, we will consider several aspects of the religious landscape that don't show up on any surveys or polls: new religious movements, or NRMs; outsider religions, a term I use to describe those highly individual religious mavericks who live and move and have their being on the social and spiritual margins of society; and the powerful influence of religion, especially conservative evangelical Christianity, in the public spheres of politics and popular culture.

New religious movements

New religious movements, or NRMs, are never entirely new. No religion is born *ex nihilo*, out of nothing. New religious movements involve a combination of *emergence and divergence* in relation to preexisting religious traditions. They *emerge* out of other religious traditions and bear the influences of those traditions, yet they also *diverge* far enough that they are no longer identified with their religious roots.

Considered in this light, all religions begin as NRMs. Buddhism was an NRM emerging and diverging from other Indian religious traditions (lumped together in modern times as Hinduism). The Baha'i Faith was an NRM emerging and diverging from Shi'ite Islam in nineteenth-century Persia (including Christian influences as well). Christianity was an NRM (the "Jesus movement") emerging and diverging from ancient Israelite and, to a lesser extent, Greco-Roman religious traditions. So was rabbinic Judaism, which became the normative form of Judaism by the second century CE.

Many, many religious movements have emerged out of Christian tradition, especially its Protestant veins, even as these movements ultimately diverge enough from that tradition to be considered, by themselves and/or by outsiders, to be new religions rather than simply denominations. Examples include the United Society of Believers in Christ's Second Appearing (aka the Shakers), Jehovah's Witness, the Church of Jesus Christ of Latter-day Saints (Mormonism), and the Church of Jesus Christ, Scientist, all of which have their deepest roots in American Protestant Christianity.

America has proven to be especially fertile ground for NRMs. Why? No doubt the answer goes back to founding national principles, especially religious freedom and the establishment in the First Amendment of a "wall of separation" between church and state. As we'll see in chapter 3, these principles were driven by a widely shared Protestant Christian individualism. Add to this the core value of dissent and rebellion, which was given foundational expression in the Declaration of Independence, along with the abundance of available land, from colonial times to the present, and you have excellent conditions for the birth of new religious movements.

Another factor is suppression. As historian of American alternative religions Stephen J. Stein makes especially clear, dissent has been better tolerated in political matters than in religious ones. Evidence abounds, from the persecutions of Anne Lee and her Shakers in the eighteenth century to the siege and tragic mass murder/suicide of David Koresh and his Branch Davidians in 1993. Intolerance of new religious movements, often demonized as "cults" by mainstream religious spokespersons, has been a consistent feature of American religious history.

Yet, despite unrelenting persecution, there has never been a slowdown in the emergence and growth of NRMs in America. As of 1995, according to J. Gordon Melton, about half of the roughly 1,500 religious groups in America were "nonconventional," and most of those would be considered NRMs. Perhaps there is something about this history of social and political suppression, ironically situated within a general Protestant-inspired American ethos valorizing individualism and religious freedom from oppression, that contributes to or even inspires their growth. Perhaps, like the Hebrew babies born into slavery in Pharaoh's Egypt, the more they are pressed down, the more they rise up and flourish.

New religious movements are often very unstable, in large part because they tend to form around charismatic individuals who claim to have special revelations. One might enjoy a mercuric rise only to disappear, almost without a trace, within a few years. Another might last exactly as long as its charismatic leader lives, or until she or he has another revelation that trumps the original. In some cases, pressure from outsiders can contribute to tragic demise, as was the case with David Koresh's movement. Among most NRMs with staying power, however, there tends to be a progression from *marginal newness to mainstream maturity*. Much like the early Jesus movement in the first and second centuries, as these new religious movements grow in numbers and stability, they develop constitutions and organizational hierarchies that facilitate their assimilation within larger social and governmental structures. Mormonism and the Jehovah's Witness are good examples.

The cultural revolution of the 1960s, combined with immigration policy changes that opened the doors to growing numbers of people identified with non-Western religious traditions, created ideal conditions for the emergence of a great many new religious movements. Steven Stein provides helpful introductions to several of them. We'll briefly examine four of his examples plus a fifth that he does not examine, the Aryan Nations, which I have researched more extensively. In the process of considering these five NRMs, we'll gain some sense of the wide variety of new religious movements in America and identify some of their most common features and patterns of development.

The International Society for Krishna Consciousness (ISKCON),

nicknamed the Hare Krishnas for their common chant, began in 1965 when a sixty-nine-year-old Indian businessman named Swami Prabhupada moved to New York and attracted a small group of disciples devoted to the service of the Hindu god Krishna. He and his group soon moved to San Francisco, where a young, countercultural ethos proved highly conducive to the growth of his movement. He established a communal structure, in which members were called to radical conversion from their former lives. They lived together in ashrams, sharing all possessions, abstaining from meat, drugs, and alcohol (as well as sex if they were unmarried), and devoting themselves entirely to Krishna consciousness, proclaiming him as supreme god of the universe. Dressed in saffron robes, they chanted and danced in the streets while distributing literature about the movement, attracting more converts, and collecting donations. After six months of these devotional practices, a member would be renamed and dedicated to lifelong service. When Prabhupada died in 1977, ISKCON reorganized itself with a board of directors. In its heyday, there were as many as 5,000 members in the United States. Today, there are probably about 3,000, with about 8,000 worldwide.

The Unification Church,

originally called the Holy Spirit Association for the Unification of World Christianity, emerged under the leadership of a North Korean minister and preacher named Sun Yung Moon (thus the religion's disparaging nickname, "Moonies"). Steeped in a Pentecostal form of Presbyterianism, Moon was imprisoned for ten years in North Korea for preaching his vision, revealed to him by Jesus Christ, that he was to help bring about the kingdom of God on earth. After his imprisonment, he published *The Divine le*, in which he laid out his vision in detail, including his interpretation of the Christian Scriptures. He argued that us was not meant to die and that his crucifixion cut short his ork of restoring the kingdom of God. A second messiah must come and finish the work. Moon believes that he and his church are ushering in the new messianic age. Members of the Unification Church believe that Moon himself is the messiah. Although Moon and his followers acknowledge that his interpretation of Christian Scriptures is unorthodox, they nonetheless see themselves as true Christians. "I can understand why Christians call us heretics," Moon once remarked in a 1977 interview with Frederick Sontag. "But most important, who will God call a heretic?"

The Church of Scientology

began with a book. In 1950, WWII veteran and science fiction enthusiast L. Ron Hubbard published *Dianetics: The Modern Science of Mental Health*, which combined theological, psychological, and contemporary scientific research to develop what he called a "science of mind" that promised an alternative means of achieving mental and spiritual health in the modern world. Its central claim was that one's true self is realized by an "auditing" therapy that exposes unconscious memories, called engrams, and allows rational reflection on them. In the auditing process, one gains conscious control of mind/spirit and body, thereby overcoming psychosomatic sufferings. Auditing involves a machine called an E-Meter that looks like a lie detector. Appealing especially to fellow science fiction readers, *Dianetics* was a best seller in 1951. Hubbard quickly established centers of research and public relations. In 1953, his movement was formally established as the Church of Scientology. Since Hubbard's death in 1986, and despite troubles with the Food and Drug Administration (concerning the E-Meter), not to mention close examination by that other auditing machine, the Internal Revenue Service, the Church of Scientology has continued to grow.

The Nation of Islam (NOI),

sometimes referred to as the Black Muslim movement, got its sta
around 1930 in Detroit with a door-to-door salesman called Wallac
Fard, later known as Master Fard Muhammad, who preached (also
door-to-door) an unorthodox form of Islam. He proclaimed the
black race to be the chosen people of Allah, opposed by the demonic
white race, and he called for a separate black nation. Fard
disappeared mysteriously in 1934 and was soon replaced by
his former head minister, Elijah Poole, renamed Elijah Muhammad.
As Supreme Minister, Elijah Muhammad led the growing movement
until his death in 1975. Promotion of the NOI was greatly assisted by
other leaders, including Malcolm X, who converted while in prison
and became one of Muhammad's key spokespersons after his release
in 1952. Other prominent NOI members include Louis Farrakhan,
who joined the movement in 1955, and Muhammad Ali (formerly
Cassius Clay), who joined in 1964 (both Ali and X eventually left
the NOI; and it is likely that X's public criticisms of Muhammad's
illicit affairs led to his assassination in 1965). Elijah Muhammad
died in 1975. His son and successor, Wallace D. Muhammad,
disagreed with many tenets of his father's movement, perceiving
its religious black supremacism and separatism to be far afield of
traditional Islam. Within a short time, Wallace had radically
reformed the movement, bringing it into the fold of orthodox
Islam, with a primary focus on reading the Qur'an and observing
the Five Pillars. He renamed the movement the American Muslim
Mission and eventually dissolved it entirely, calling for his followers
to become part of Islam proper. Under the leadership of Louis
Farrakhan, dissenters from Wallace D. Muhammad's reformed
movement formed a new Nation of Islam, harkening back to the
previous generation.

With the Nation of Islam, we get an inkling of the potential for
militant revolutionary radicalism in some American NRMs. With
our final example, below, we get much more than an inkling.

3. Elijah Muhammad (1897–1975), Supreme Minister of the Nation of Islam, addresses followers, including Cassius Clay, aka Muhammad Ali, 1964. Ali and others, including Malcolm X, eventually left the Nation of Islam.

Aryan Nations

is a radical white supremacist religious movement founded by Richard G. Butler as the political wing of the Church of Jesus Christ-Christian. Butler was steeped in the theology of Christian Identity, a form of Anglo-Israelism that believes that white Europeans are the true descendents of the lost northern tribes of ancient Israel and that Jewish people are not descended from Adam but from Satan. According to this racist theology, Jews are believed to have usurped the status as children of God and have come to control most of the world through what they call the ZOG, or Zionist Occupied Government. Although better known for their white racism against black people, the core of their beliefs is more directly anti-Semitic.

Butler established his headquarters on wooded property near Hayden Lake, Idaho, in 1974. With its church, meeting houses, and

open land for various military exercises and religious rit...
compound soon became a mecca for white supremacists o...
stripes, unified in their focus on a common enemy, the ZOG...
their apocalyptic vision of history as a racial holy war.

In 2001, a woman and her teenaged son who had been violently
harassed by guards at the Hayden Lake compound brought a
lawsuit against Butler, as head of the Aryan Nations. Supported by
the Southern Poverty Law Center, they won the suit. Butler's
organization was bankrupted, and he lost the Hayden Lake
property. Butler, then in his eighties, began to lose control of the
movement. He died in 2004, leaving it in a state of leaderless
diaspora, with several radical protégés struggling for preeminence
(some with far more radically militant tendencies and histories of
violence than Butler). Most recently, the organization appears to
have embraced its leaderless, decentralized state and has
essentially dissolved itself into a "permanent policy of
decentralization and leaderless resistance under the radical banner
of pan-Aryanism," which it describes as the global, revolutionary
struggle against what it believes to be a Jewish conspiracy of
Satanic world domination. Since 9/11, moreover, the organization
has been especially active in forming bonds with radical Islamist
organizations that share its religious anti-Semitism, conspiracy
theories, and apocalyptic vision of history as a cosmic struggle
between good and evil.

Although the examples briefly described here are each unique in
many respects, they nonetheless reveal several common hallmarks
of NRMs in America.

First, NRMs often originate with a single, charismatic leader who
claims to have had a special revelation. If the movement continues
beyond the lifespan of its leader, her or his new revelations may
become a scripture (often taking the form of a secondary canon
to supplement a more traditional one, such as the Qur'an or the
Christian Bible).

RMs often set themselves apart through the promotion
ernative, countercultural worldview. Often this worldview
calyptic, envisioning the present time in terms of a cosmic
le between good and evil, with the masses taking the wrong
le unawares. The NRM offers critique of mainstream, mass
culture, which is being duped by evil powers (thus Sun Yung
Moon's question, "Who will God call a heretic?"; and the
conspiracy theories of the Aryan Nations and Nation of Islam).

Third, and relatedly, one often gains membership in the NRM only
by way of a radical conversion, in which she or he breaks
definitively from mainstream society and its values. Here ascetic
practices of self-denial and voluntary poverty may come into play
(e.g., ISKCON). More radical, even violent actions against the
dominant powers that be may also be encouraged, if not required.

Fourth, NRMs in America often incorporate elements that have
been imported from less familiar, non-Western religious
traditions. Indeed, these elements often immigrate to the United
States *along with* the NRM's leader (e.g., Swami Prabhupada).
Since the Immigration and Nationality Act of 1965, and in the
wake of the cultural revolution of the 1960s, elements of religious
traditions from Asia have been especially influential on the
emergence of many NRMs.

In light of these hallmarks, especially the first three, it is no surprise
that many NRMs in America have aroused suspicion, not only from
mainline ecclesiastical authorities, who describe them pejoratively as
"cults," but also from federal and state governments. In fact, the best
source of information on some NRMs (such as the Aryan Nations
and the Nation of Islam) is the FBI via the Freedom of Information
Act. Too often, however, this kind of attention from "intelligence"
and law enforcement authorities, combined with demonizing
stereotypes promoted in many churches, has led to tragic face-offs, as
was the case in the 1978 mass murder-and-suicide at Jonestown,
Guyana, and the 1993 siege against the Branch Davidians.

Outsider religion

No survey of religion in America would be complete without at least a passing look at those highly individual, often disturbingly peculiar religious expressions that dot the landscape. *Roadside Religion* tells the story of my own exploration of many such religious spectacles, from handmade re-creations of the biblical Holy Land in the Blue Ridge mountains of Virginia to slick, Disneyesque versions in Orlando, Florida, to the World's Largest Ten Commandments in North Carolina to a life-sized Noah's ark under construction in Maryland to Precious Moments Inspiration Park in Missouri to the World's Largest Rosary Collection in Washington State—to name a few. Let's consider briefly two examples, one from my book and another that I've only recently discovered.

In 1977 Howard Finster was in his backyard in Summerville, Georgia, touching up a scratch on an old bicycle, when he saw a face appear in the paint on his index finger.

"Paint sacred art," it said.

To which this sixty-year-old itinerant Baptist preacher and sometime handyman replied that he couldn't because he was not an artist.

"How do you know?" asked the face.

He found a piece of plywood, tacked a dollar bill to it, and copied George Washington's portrait.

Such is the call narrative of this religious visionary artist-preacher, and so began Paradise Gardens, a neighborhood block of sculptures, paintings, scripture boards, and chapels of all sizes that have accrued there over more than three decades. Finster, who died in 2001, proclaimed Paradise Gardens to be the center of the Folk Art Church and declared himself its minister.

ever seen a person I didn't love" is painted on an old truck bumper on stilts. Finster welcomed anyone and everyone to his folk art paradise. Pilgrims, mostly nonreligious or post-Christian young people, would come from all over the South to behold the gardens, to participate in their growth, and to hear him preach and play his banjo on his porch.

Toward the end of Finster's life, Paradise Gardens had fallen into disrepair. In recent years, however, his disciples and children have dedicated themselves to its nurture, and to Finster's memory.

For Finster and his friends, this garden of handmade religious art is paradise regained. In biblical tradition, the garden of paradise was the place of original divine creation, where God made humankind in God's own image. In Paradise Gardens, to be creative, to make sacred art, is to be in the image of God. That was Finster's vision.

In rural Georgia, Howard Finster had plenty of private property on which to grow and expand his Edenic vision. In a densely populated urban environment, different strategies of religious expression are necessary. Such was the case for the late Reverend Albert Wagner, whose small house on a postage stamp of land in East Cleveland is filled, from basement to attic, with his visionary artwork.

Wagner's house is itself a work of religious art and hospitality. Its two second-story windows have been made to look like eyes and a trunklike nose has been attached in the center. His art, which has in recent years drawn attention from folk art enthusiasts, represents a hybrid mix of Christian, Jewish, and African influences (Wagner himself is African American). Moses in Egypt (northern Africa) is a prominent theme. In some works, the Egyptian Pharaoh's daughter who, according to Exodus, raised Moses from infancy, is depicted as an African Madonna holding the future deliverer.

4. Pickup camper turned sacred art at Howard Finster's Paradise Gardens, a neighborhood block of religiously inspired outsider art in Summerville, Georgia. Finster, who died in 2001, called himself the "The World's Minister of the Folk Art Church."

Until his death in 2006, Reverend Wagner was an active preacher, holding services in his basement on Saturdays for his very large extended family and neighbors (as many as 100 people would gather there for hours of singing, testimonials, and preaching). Devoted to the support and pastoral care of the poor and struggling in East Cleveland, he called his church the People Love People House of God. His children now continue this ministry of hospitality. The doors of the Wagner house are always open.

In the art world, "outsider artists" are those without formal training or access to high-culture museums and galleries. Bearing little or no relation to trends and developments in the fine art world, outsider artists stand on the social and conceptual fringes of American culture. Likewise, I suggest that we seriously consider the highly individual, highly peculiar religious lives, works, and

s of outsider artists like Finster and Wagner as examples
…ider religion."

…pressions of outsider religion such as these operate in tensions
…etween the private and the public. They are very outward, public
expressions of very inward, private religious visions. At the creative
heart and soul of each is a religious imagination trying to give
outward form to inner experience. Each is a creative public
response to a profoundly life-changing personal experience. There's
something about that experience that won't let go, that insists on
being communicated, translated to others in spectacular form.

It's no coincidence that most of these roadside religious spectacles
are also private homes. In one sense, this is simply a practical
matter. One starts where one is, and most of these people aren't
rich or fundraising-savvy enough to consider other locations.
But I think there's more to it than that. On the one hand, a home
is private property, protected space, a shelter from the storm,
a locus of intimacy and secrets. On the other hand, it's a public
expression of oneself, an address where people can find you,
a place of hospitality, for welcoming strangers. Home is both
private and public, individual and social. So, too, the outsider
religious spaces of individuals like Finster and Wagner.

Religion in pop culture and politics

To get the "big picture" of religion in America, we must also
consider the powerful influence of religion, especially
evangelical Protestant Christianity, in the public sphere.
It pervades popular media, from huge best sellers like Tim
F. LaHaye's *Left Behind* series of end-times Christian thrillers
and Rick Warren's *The Purpose Driven Life*, which has spawned
a multimillion-dollar industry of Christian education and
spiritual development curricula and programming, to blockbuster
movies like Mel Gibson's *The Passion of the Christ*. But its

influence reaches far beyond that of explicitly religious po[...]
media. It's doubtful that Janet Jackson's breast-baring "war[...]
malfunction" during the halftime show of Superbowl XXVIII
would have generated such a massive public outcry in any other
country. Contrast Canada, where it also aired: whereas the Federa[...]
Communications Commission received more than a half million
complaints about the incident, the Canadian Broadcast Standards
Council received about fifty.

Even unorthodox religious media phenomena such as Dan Brown's
The DaVinci Code, which offers a more and less fictional
alternative to established doctrines about the life of Jesus and the
formation of the Bible, presume and depend on the massive
influence of conservative Christianity on popular culture as the
means of their divergence. It would not have succeeded so
phenomenally if it had not appeared to present an alternative
vision of Christianity, purportedly suppressed by a massive Roman
Catholic conspiracy. So too when it comes to many books and
shows that are openly antagonistic toward conservative
Christianity, such as the cartoon *South Park*, which has been
poking fun at sacred traditions since its pilot episode, "The Spirit
of Christmas," which featured a death match between Jesus and
Santa Claus in a shopping mall. Some might suggest that the
success of shows like *South Park* indicates that the Puritanical grip
on popular culture is loosening. Yet their humor derives largely
from pushing, adolescent-style, against its scolding predominance.
Thus they are symptomatic of the general conservative Christian
ethos. It's their reason for being.

These days, moreover, we have all grown very aware of how
politically charged religion in America is. Conservative Christian
values organizations are the primary movers on numerous fronts
that concern specific policy issues: abortion, stem cell research,
prayer in schools, teaching "intelligent design" as an alternative to
evolution in science classrooms, and so on. There has never been a
non-Christian president of the United States, and all save one

ly) have been Protestant. No doubt Mitt Romney's run for
Republican nomination in 2008 was hurt by his Mormonism,
ch steered many conservative Christian voters toward other
ndidates like Baptist preacher Mike Huckabee.

Since the contested win of George W. Bush over Al Gore in 2004,
the general public has become much more aware of the
conservative, Republican-leaning "evangelical vote," which most
consider to have been the deciding factor in that election. But the
influence of evangelical Christianity in election politics has been
building for decades. Ironically, it was a liberal Democrat, Jimmy
Carter, who first "came out" as an evangelical Christian in an
election. "The most important thing in my life," he often said during
his 1976 campaign, "is Jesus Christ." Describing himself as an
evangelical, born-again Christian—language that was at the time
unfamiliar in mainstream news—Carter earned the endorsements
of several prominent evangelical leaders. At the 1976 Southern
Baptist Convention, he was introduced as the only candidate whose
"initials are the same as our Lord's." He easily won the election,
earning more than 50 percent of the evangelical vote.

As president, however, Carter's support of the Equal Rights
Amendment, the Roe *v.* Wade decision, and other progressive
initiatives, alienated him from many conservative Christians.
Disappointed in him but bolstered by a new sense of political and
power and influence, charismatic Christian media entrepreneurs
and televangelists like Pat Robertson, James Robison, and Jerry
Falwell began to organize themselves politically into what come to
be known as the New Christian Right.

The most powerful organization was Falwell's Moral Majority,
founded in 1979 with the political goal of unifying and mobilizing
evangelical voters—as well as like-minded nonevangelicals—to
remove Carter from office and deliver a president, congress, and
Supreme Court that would help legislate their agenda, which
included outlawing abortion, encouraging public prayer in schools,

and supporting traditional, patriarchal family values. Falw[...] famously declared three priorities for all Americans: to be sa[...] to be baptized, and to vote. In that order.

Ronald Reagan's catering to the Moral Majority and other conservative evangelical leaders won him the presidency in 1980, and the New Christian Right was born. The current president, George W. Bush, himself a born-again evangelical Christian with an agenda explicitly in line with Christian Rightist organizations, is its greatest success.

5. Jerry Falwell whispering in Ronald Reagan's ear during the 1980 presidential campaign. Falwell's Moral Majority and related organizations were instrumental in electing Reagan over Jimmy Carter, who had lost their favor on account of his views concerning abortion and women's rights.

Recently, however, many evangelicals are questioning the
Christian Right's close alliance with political power. Believing that
Christians must maintain a prophetic voice, speaking truth to
power even when it might marginalize them, a growing number of
evangelical leaders are asking whether they have compromised
certain core Gospel values, including responsibility to the poor and
the oppressed and stewardship of the environment.

An American paradox

E Pluribus Unum, "from many, one." This motto first appeared
on a banner in the beak of a bald eagle on the Great Seal of the
United States, adopted in 1782, and it has appeared on the back
of every American coin since 1873. There are other mottos on
the Great Seal: *Novus Ordo Seclorum*, "new order of the ages,"
and *Annuit Coeptis*, "favored undertakings," suggesting divine
providential oversight of the young nation. And there were
other mottos proposed by American founders that didn't make
the cut, among them, "Rebellion to Tyrants is Obedience to God."
(Imagine if that one had been adopted!) But it is the declaration
of *E Pluribus Unum*, the affirmation of unity from, and
in, plurality, that has taken hold as a banner of American
idealism.

This is no simple declaration. Embodied in it is a deep and abiding paradox that goes to the very heart of religion in America: an affirmation of *both* the *one* and the *many*, of unity and plurality, of collective identity and individual difference, of conformity and dissent.

The paradoxical embrace of these two opposing values, so succinctly put in this motto, has everything to do with what makes religion in America so uniquely fascinating, and perplexing. On the one hand, there is a powerful, predominantly Protestant, conservative Christian mainstream of beliefs and values, often bringing along with it those religious Americans who are not Christian but share many of its moral and political interests. The powerful influence of the Christian Right is the most obvious example. On the other hand, as we have seen, America is rich in highly particular, often highly peculiar religious groups and individuals that stand well beyond the mainstream: from the many denominational splinters, and splinters of splinters, of mainline Protestantism to outsider religious personalities like the Reverends Howard Finster and Albert Wagner whose creative ministries decorate our highways, byways, and alleyways, to NRMs like Scientology and ISKCON, and the Aryan Nations.

What aspects of religious history have made American soil so fertile for such a rich paradox? And how will the revolutionary forces that are transforming the American religious landscape today shape its future?

Chapter 3
Looking Back
Uneasy Inheritances

There is no grand narrative of religion in America, no founding myth, no single common story of "us," which might ground American religious identity. There are, rather, many little stories, often circling around the same people and events of the past but taking very different, even conflicting, perspectives on them. We might think of them as family stories about great-grandparents who are "mixed bags," whose occasional nobility and passion for justice might make you proud one minute, while their moral lapses and selfish prejudices make you cringe in shame and inherited guilt the next. Our legacy of American religious history is at least as messy. There are many closets full of many skeletons, most of which we no longer even recognize.

When we make stories, we make meaning that wasn't simply there to discover. We choose which elements to include, which to exclude, which to highlight, and how to reshape them so that they fit within a larger narrative whole. There are always elements of the past that don't fit. Often, these "other" bits and accursed shares of our past are the very things that most demand our ethical attention.

Historians of religion in America must always grapple with a problem. How to attend to those *little stories*, as philosopher Je François Lyotard called them (*petit récits*), those anomalous bits the past that call into question the grand narrative, be it the narrative of a nation, a people, or an individual. For the history of religion in America is not a tall tale of progress toward the fulfillment of an ideal. It is, rather, a past riddled with conflicts involving countless experiences and perspectives, a cacophony of voices, and haunted by the silences of many other voices that are lost forever, without an echo.

Here we look back on three historical influences that continue to shape religion in America today: the dispossession of Native Americans and their indigenous religious traditions; the struggle for religious freedom; and revivalism and the rise of a uniquely American evangelical consciousness. As we delve into each, we will try to avoid the temptation to integrate them into a grand narrative of our patriarchal heroes of religious freedom and tolerance. Instead, we will explore them as controversial issues, uneasy inheritances, reflecting on how each of them continues to inspire, and haunt, religion in America to this day.

Possession and dispossession: religion in Native America

Nowadays, the Rockwellian image of a dining room table dressed for Thanksgiving is a veritable icon of religion in America. For many, it quickens feelings of abundant harvest, gratefully received. It's an almost sacramental remembrance of America's mythical beginnings, awakening nostalgia for pristine origins, a time of hard work and bounty shared in peace between "us" the Puritan newcomers and "them" the Native Americans.

Events that we charge with such a sense of perfect fulfillment and celebratory memory are always, on another level, riddled with ambivalences, doubts, lingering disappointments. Thanksgiving is

...eption. Between courses, smiles for the camera, ...ecoming prayers, and post-pie tummy pats, we are aware of ...tain uneasy, mixed feelings, not only about the abundance we ...roclaim and the family bliss we pretend but also the national, founding story we celebrate.

For a minority of Americans, in fact, Thanksgiving is a day not for celebration but for mourning. Theirs is the indigenous, Native American version of the story, the story of conquest and dispossession by Western European immigrants of indigenous communities that had lived and thrived in America for centuries.

This story begins before Christopher Columbus had spent a single night in the "New Land." On October 12, 1492, Columbus reported in his journal that he and members of his crew "saw naked people" on the shoreline as they landed in their armed launch. Columbus jumped ashore and, with his two other captains as witnesses, declared that he would take possession of the island for King Ferdinand and Queen Isabella.

The "naked people" who gathered around Columbus and his crew were the Taino Arawak, natives of the island that the Spaniards called Hispaniola (now Haiti and the Dominican Republic). Columbus described them as very warm and friendly, peaceful, and generous with all their possessions. Reflecting on their friendly naïveté, Columbus concludes, "They should be good and intelligent slaves." A few days later, he suggested that the entire population be taken to Castile or held captive, "because with 50 men all of them could be held in subjection and can be made to do whatever one might wish."

Columbus's contemporary, Bartolemé de Las Casas, gives a firsthand account of how Columbus and many other Spaniards did in fact kidnap, torture, and enslave many of these natives, and killed many more in their pursuit of gold. Casas described unimaginable horrors as the conquistadors attacked defenseless

> They do not carry arms nor are they acquainted with them, because I showed them swords and they took them by the edge and through ignorance cut themselves. . . . All of them alike are of good-sized stature and carry themselves well. I saw some who had marks of wounds on their bodies and I made signs to them asking them what they were; and they showed me how people from other islands nearby came there and tried to take them, and how they defended themselves; and I believed and believe that they come here from tierra firme to take them by captive. They should be good and intelligent servants, for I see that they say very quickly everything that is said to them; and I believe they would become Christians very easily, for it seemed to me that they had no religion.
>
> —Christopher Columbus's *Diario*, October 12, 1492

villages like "ravenous beasts," slaying all who tried to defend themselves and enslaving the countless others who survived. Fifty years after Columbus' "discovery" of Hispaniola and its nearby islands, Casas estimated that only five hundred of the once thriving population survived.

This story of brutal dispossession and exploitation would be repeated many times throughout the next three centuries, as armed groups of Europeans, calling themselves Christians, came west to the shores of the Americas seeking slaves, gold, fur, and other fortunes. Native American populations were also decimated by imported strains of disease to which they had no immunity.

With the introduction of firearms, moreover, struggles between tribes and with European settlers were far more devastating. Conflicts between colonial settlers and native populations, known as the Indian Wars, continued from the 1600s through the 1800s, as settlers pressed westward for more and more land, and struggled for national independence and unity.

In fact, both the American Revolutionary War and the War of 1812 were fought on two fronts. There was the eastern front, against the British. But there was also the western front, against the Native Americans, many of which were allied with the British, who had maintained more peaceful relations with them (in 1763, for example, they had enacted a law prohibiting the westward expansion of settlers beyond the Appalachian Mountains). In both wars, however, the British eventually abandoned their Native American allies, paving the way for President Andrew Jackson's Indian Removal Act of 1830, which authorized him to negotiate treaties that claimed tribal lands in the east and relocated native populations to land acquired in the Louisiana Purchase. Interestingly, Jackson justified this act on the basis of national security interests. Done for the sake of homeland security.

Some Native American peoples in the south (Florida, Georgia, Alabama, and Mississippi) resisted, but the U.S. armies ultimately prevailed. The historian Russell Thornton estimates that in the forty wars waged between 1775 and 1890 (the massacre at Wounded Knee), about 45,000 Indians and 19,000 colonials, including many women and children, were killed. By the end, nearly all Native American groups had been forced to assimilate or move to reservations.

A grim and shameful story indeed. It is not an exaggeration to describe what happened as ethnic cleansing.

One of the reasons that the story went this way had to do with the religious self-understanding of the settlers. From the beginning of the colonial period in the early 1600s, they believed themselves to be part of a story of biblical proportions. According to their fantasy drama, they were the chosen people, the New Israel, entering a land of milk and honey promised to them by God. The indigenous peoples were forced to play the biblical role of the Canaanites. By divine right, the new Israelites were to conquer and drive them out. Manifest Destiny.

> Captaine Smith, you may understand that I having seene the
> death of all my people thrice, and not any one living of these
> three generations but my selfe; I know the difference of Peace
> and Warre better then any in my Country. . . . What will it availe
> you to take that by force you may quickly have by love, or to
> destroy them that provide you food. What can you get by warre,
> when we can hide our provisions and fly to the woods? whereby
> you must famish by wronging us your friends. And why are you
> thus jealous of our loves seeing us unarmed, and both doe, and
> are willing still to feede you, with that you cannot get but by our
> labours?
>
> —Chief Powhatan to Captain John Smith, 1608, as remembered by Smith

This sense of divinely ordained right to possess the new land, and
in the process to dispossess its indigenous peoples, was bolstered
by the political theology of the late seventeenth-century
philosopher John Locke in his *Two Treatises on Government*. We
are used to hearing his name in the context of the American
struggle for independence from Great Britain; indeed, he was
something of an intellectual patron saint among the early
"founding fathers" of the United States, having provided much of
the key language for the Declaration of Independence concerning
limited government and the right to revolution. Less familiar to
many these days, however, is Locke's similarly influential doctrine
of the natural human right to possess private property.

Based on an interpretation of the biblical creation story, Locke
argued that labor *invests* ownership in property. To work the land
and make it produce is to lay claim to it. "His labour hath taken it
out of the hands of nature, where it was common, and belonged
equally to all her children, and hath thereby appropriated it to
himself. . . . He by his labour does, as it were, inclose it from the
common."

According to Locke's doctrine, the Native Americans appeared to be failing to take full advantage of the land as resource, through their labor. Viewed through a Lockean lens, American land on which natives had lived for many centuries appeared to be a "vacant" expanse of "wild woods and uncultivated waste." They seemed to be wasting it and therefore forfeiting their claim to it as property.

That this conception of the use-value of nature as private property was completely foreign to Native American populations mattered little to the settlers. Few early settlers or government officials had any appreciation for the indigenous religious conceptions of this land that had taken root and developed there over centuries.

Native American historian, political advocate, and religious scholar Vine Deloria Jr. presented this uniquely American problem in the most provocative terms. The struggle between Native Americans and European settlers, he argued, was essentially a religious one, between a Native American religion rooted in geography (relationship with the land as sacred) and a European Christian religion rooted in an idea of history (divinely sanctioned conquest). As the struggle continued, indeed escalated, after the American Revolution, Indians were projected as the United States' "other," the not-us that threatened unity.

From the beginning, America's embrace of religious diversity was an anxious embrace, for all were aware that that same diversity threatened unity. There were in fact many potentially explosive differences within those young United States, even and especially among those groups identified with Protestant Christianity, and disputes between them often turned violent.

American Indians repeatedly became the scapegoat for those anxieties. They were projected as the inassimilable "other within," that element of the *pluribus* that threatened "our" *unum*. In this dynamic, we recognize the social value of othering: it creates a

⇒ Power of the "other?"

collective feeling of unity over against a shared "not-us." Native Americans were put in the role of the other that could potentially unsettle the precarious unity of the young and still very unstable United States of America. Thus Jackson's national security rationale for the Removal Act.

This treatment of the American Indian as both political and religious other to the United States continued well into the twentieth century. In fact, their otherness was often described primarily in religious terms. And remember, American Indians were not given citizenship, guaranteeing their constitutional right to religious freedom, until the Indian Citizenship Act of 1924.

As late as 1921, the Office of Indian Affairs issued a circular that explicitly prohibited Indian "so-called religious ceremonies," continuing to describe them as "Indian Offences." In 1923 Commissioner Charles Burke, the author of the circular, followed up

> I feel that something must be done to stop the neglect of stock, crops, gardens, and home interests caused by these dances or by celebrations, pow-wows, and gatherings of any kind that take the time of the Indians for many days. Now, what I want you to think about very seriously is that you must first of all try to make your own living, which you cannot do unless you work faithfully and take care of what comes from your labor, and go to dances or other meetings only when your home work will not suffer by it. I do not want to deprive you of decent amusements or occasional feast days, but you should not do evil or foolish things or take so much time for these occasions. No good comes from your "give-away" custom at dances and it should be stopped. . . . All such extreme things are wrong and should be put aside and forgotten.
>
> —Letter "To All Indians" from Charles Burke, Commissioner of the Office of Indian Affairs, 1923

with a patronizing letter addressed "To All Indians." Writing in a condescending tone, as though to misbehaving children, he begged them to discontinue their ceremonial dances and rituals, including "give-aways" of property and other valuables to one another, and to give more attention to productive labor on their land.

Notice how Burke's criticisms of their religious practices presume Lockean conceptions of property and productive labor. Burke's efforts to assimilate Native American religious and economic practices with the dominant Western European culture are part of a struggle that goes back to the very beginnings of the United States of America.

Whether Burke understood that the government's opposition to their practices was deeply and fundamentally religious, Native Americans certainly did. John Collier, founder of the American Indian Defense Association, made this understanding very clear. In response to Burke, he wrote:

> Now today, this late date, the Indian Bureau has commenced a new onslaught. The Indians are deeply and universally religious. They still know how as tribes to follow ancient paths leading to the water of heaven. United in this life of religion, they can still stand up together as men, and they can still cling to their coveted remnants of soil. They can resist the efforts to turn them into drifting social half-breeds slave-driven by 6,000 Indian Bureau job holders who make their living "civilizing" the Indians. Therefore, an actual inquisition shall be elaborated against their adult worship. Their treasure of the soul which no man yet has known enough to be able to estimate shall be forcibly thrown away; their last liberty and last dignity and their end of life, which they know to be God, shall be denied (as quoted by Dwight Dutschke).

Over the past few decades, since the cultural revolutions of the sixties, there has been far more popular interest in Native American religion among non-Native Americans. Much of this interest is explicitly in reaction to Protestant American religious heritage. A growing number feel that that heritage has become too closely identified with nationalism, power politics, and consumer culture. People seeking non-Western, alternative forms of spirituality often see in Native American religion a possible means of reconnecting with nature and geography. One must ask whether this newfound interest among many whites also reflects a certain sense of nostalgia for that which has been lost, as well as a sense of inherited guilt and sorrow for the decimation of these indigenous religious cultures by their colonial ancestors. Native Americans today are justified to see this new interest as too little too late.

In *Custer Died for Your Sins: An Indian Manifesto*, Deloria showed how even ostensibly well-meaning interest in their culture and religion among non-Native American scholars often inadvertently continues the long history of exploitation, even and especially through idealizations of them as the West's other. Such representations, no matter how well intended, have "contributed substantially to the invisibility of Indian people today." He argued that any involvement with Native Americans today must speak to the interests of Native Americans themselves, rather than claiming to speak or act *for* them.

The long, mean history of Native American dispossession haunts not only the current political landscape of the United States but also its religious landscape, much as Nazism and the Holocaust haunt the current German political and religious landscape. The past lives on in the present, and there is no obvious way to come to terms with it.

Revolution and religious freedom

In many respects, religion and politics in America have never been separate. From the beginnings of the earliest colonies, the desire for religious freedom among groups like Puritans, fleeing persecution and disenfranchisement in England, was a strong motivation.

6. Hopi "war" dance demonstration outside the U.S. Capitol, 1926. Indigenous Native American religion and the terrible history of its erasure continue to haunt today's religious landscape.

Yet the survival of these groups in the "new world" depended heavily on the economic and political interests of the European empires that maintained close relations with them. The opportunity to practice their faith as they were so led depended on their willing economic bondage to kings and queens back home. When, in 1691, the Reverend James Blair went to England to request that a university be established in Virginia, because Virginians have souls too, the treasury commissioner, Sir Edward Seymour, replied, "Souls! Damn your souls. Make Tobacco." Blair eventually founded the College of William and Mary, but this first response from Seymour speaks volumes about the complex relationship between religious and economic dependence and independence in the colonies.

The earliest Puritan settlers, moreover, did not separate church and state in their own self-governance. They sought to implement a form of government in which religious and civil authorities were simpatico. This form of theocracy, based on biblical interpretation, was given its basic outline in John Winthrop's *A Model of Christian Charity*, which he wrote in 1630 while sailing to the shores of Massachusetts on the *Arbella* with a group of Puritans. There he envisioned the new community in terms of the biblical metaphor of the church as the body of Christ, in which all members work together in justice and mercy on behalf of the whole.

From the beginning, there were arguments within this theocratic framework about the extent of civil authority in matters of religion. John Cotton (1584–1652) was an outspoken advocate for uniting both the voice of the church and the sword of the state to enforce right faith and conscience. Roger Williams (1603–83), on the other hand, called for a two-fold system, with spiritual and civil states, civil and spiritual officers, and civil and spiritual weapons, "these states being of different natures and considerations, as far differing as spirit from flesh."

The War of Independence (1776–83) between Great Britain and the thirteen united colonies was a struggle for *religious* liberty as much as for national liberty. It was a rebellion against tyranny, and in the world of eighteenth-century Europe, the tyranny of bishops and popes was inextricably tied to the tyranny of princes and kings. Church and state in the old world were one. American Protestants, with a long history in England of resistance to the Roman Catholic Church and the Church of England, resisted the authority of both. And they did so on grounds that were simultaneously political and theological.

Inspiration for the popular movement toward independence was found primarily in the sermons and essays of Protestant ministers and theologians who carried the spirit of Roger Williams and others like him into the eighteenth century. Central in their arguments was the Protestant understanding of religious faith as absolutely personal. Every individual ultimately stands alone before God, accountable for her or his own faith and conscience.

The state should not try to coerce faith, which is a matter of individual free will—"soul liberty" as Williams had called it.

Grounded in this Protestant theological tradition and influenced by the liberal, "enlightened" political theology of Locke and others, colonial ministers like Jonathan Mayhew (1720–66) preached resistance to what they saw as the tandem tyranny of imperial Great Britain and the Church of England (rumored in the 1760s to be planning to bring a bishop to Boston). In the cause of liberty it was not only a right but also a duty to resist tyranny, whether its face was a prince or a bishop, and especially when the two were wed in an "impious bargain ... betwixt the scepter and the surplice, for enslaving both the bodies and souls of men."

A wall of separation

Such progressive Protestant theological arguments for individual religious liberty from civil authority were foundational not only for the cause of revolution but also for the Constitution of the United States in the decade following independence. The belief that God created human beings to have personal freedom of mind and conscience was the cornerstone of the Virginia Statute for Religious Freedom, which was written by Thomas Jefferson in 1779 and secured into state law by James Madison in 1786 (it remains part of Virginia law today). It declares that

> no man shall be compelled to frequent or support any religious worship, place, or ministry whatsoever, nor shall be enforced, restrained, molested, or burthened in his body or goods, nor shall otherwise suffer on account of his religious opinions or belief, but that all men shall be free to profess, and by argument to maintain, their opinion in matters of Religion, and that the same shall in no wise diminish, enlarge or affect their civil capacities.

In his 1785 *Memorial and Remonstrance on the Religious Rights of Man*, written against Patrick Henry's bill to establish a Virginia state tax to support religion, Madison elaborated the theological grounds of his and Jefferson's argument more fully. Echoing Mayhew and other revolutionary voices, he described personal freedom of religion as a natural human right, given by God. Religious freedom is sacrosanct, holy. "If this freedom is abused, it is an offence against God, *not against man*." Any civil authority that encroaches on this God-given right or that employs "religion as an engine of civil policy" is tyrannical. And tyrants will be accountable, above all, to God. Grounded in this theological understanding of human rights, Madison represented Henry's bill as a "melancholy mark ... of sudden degeneracy," different in degree but not in kind from the Spanish Inquisition: "the one is the *first* step, the other the *last*, in the *career of intolerance*."

The Virginia Statute and supporting *Remonstrance* stand behind the First Amendment to the Constitution (proposed in 1789 and ratified in 1791), which begins the Bill of Rights.

> Congress shall make no law respecting an establishment of religion, or prohibiting the free exercise thereof; or abridging the freedom of speech, or of the press; or the right of the people peaceably to assemble, and to petition the Government for a redress of grievances.

The first two clauses of this amendment directly concern religion. The "establishment clause" prohibits the federal government from establishing any religion as a state religion (as European states had done), and the "free exercise" clause prohibits the government from prohibiting anyone's free exercise of religion. Behind these two clauses is the modern Protestant theological emphasis on the individual conscience as the seat of religion, divinely ordained to come to faith of its own free will without the meddling of civil authority.

Note that the phrase "separation of church and state" does not appear in the First Amendment itself. It was not until 1802, in a letter that the newly elected President Jefferson wrote to a group of Baptists in Danbury, Connecticut, that the metaphorical language of a wall of separation between church and state found expression. The First Amendment, ratified a decade earlier, applied only to the federal government, not to the laws and policies of specific states, as the Danbury Baptists were only too aware. In their letter of October 1801, they complained to Jefferson that certain state practices and policies hindered their enjoyment of these rights.

> Our ancient charter together with the law made coincident therewith, were adopted as the basis of our government, at the time of our revolution; and such had been our laws and usages, and such still are; that religion is considered as the first object of legislation; and therefore what religious privileges we enjoy (as a minor part of the state) we enjoy as favors granted, and not as inalienable rights; and these favors we receive at the expense of such degrading acknowledgements as are inconsistent with the rights of freemen.

Jefferson's response on New Year's Day, 1802, was less than the Danbury Baptists must have hoped for. He reiterated his wholehearted commitment, shared with them, to the establishment and free exercise clauses of the First Amendment. Yet he stopped short of addressing directly their specific concern, which was that state laws and practices contradicted them. Along the way, however, he described the clauses as "building a wall of separation between Church & State." Although it would not be until 1868, with the Fourteenth Amendment, that state and local laws would be forced to conform to the Bill of Rights, this letter introduced language that remains central to this day concerning religion, law, and politics: the separation of church and state.

As much as we might wish it were otherwise, we find very few arguments for religious freedom motivated by any desire to promote religious diversity and hospitality to non-Christians. For many, in fact, the motives were quite the reverse: they wished to

> Believing with you that religion is a matter which lies solely between Man & his God, that he owes account to none other for his faith or his worship, that the legitimate powers of government reach actions only, & not opinions, I contemplate with sovereign reverence that act of the whole American people which declared that their legislature should "make no law respecting an establishment of religion, or prohibiting the free exercise thereof," thus building a wall of separation between Church & State.
>
> —from Thomas Jefferson's Letter to the Danbury Baptists, sent January 1, 1802

promote the rise of Christianity in America. If true and authentic Christian faith cannot be coerced but depends on the free exercise of the individual mind, then the growth of Christianity required a context of religious freedom. In this respect, many early Christian promoters of religious freedom in the new United States were not far from the young Martin Luther, who believed that Jews would convert to Christianity once they understood the Gospel message as he understood it.

There is a dark side to this kind of confidence, which often appears only when it is frustrated. Luther's disappointment in the refusal of the Gospel by Jews turned his young evangelical hopes into anti-Jewish rage, calling for the state to burn their books, defrock their leaders, and confiscate their property. Hitler's first major pogrom against Jews, *Kristalnacht* (named for the broken window glass from the Jewish homes, synagogues, and businesses), was carried out on and in commemoration of Luther's birthday.

Although the rights guaranteed in the First Amendment have, in the long run, led to unprecedented religious diversity in the United States today, such was not the intent of most of its early promoters. The legacy of ever-growing religious diversity in America over the past two centuries, and especially over the past half century, is in this respect an ironic one. Many Americans love the irony. Others do not.

Revivalism

Beholding the religious landscape of America today, most of us—and nearly all of the rest of the world—are struck by two fairly unique features of Christianity in America. One is the prevalence of a rather uniquely American evangelical consciousness that privileges conversion, religious emotion, and personal relationship with Jesus Christ, and which links religious faith to particular moral and political values to be promoted in the larger society. The other is the rapidly growing movement of Pentecostalism, by which I refer to the charismatic forms of Christianity rooted in ecstatic experience of the "gifts," or anointing, of the Holy Spirit. As we saw in chapter 2, these are the fastest growing forms of Christianity in America. Pentecostalism, moreover, is America's number one religious export.

To understand the development of these made-in-America forms of Christianity, we need to look back into the history of revivalism in America, beginning with the first Great Awakening.

Great awakenings

In the 1730s and 1740s a series of Christian revivals swept the Middle Colonies and New England like wildfire. Known at the time as the "great and general revival of religion," this era has come to be known by historians as the Great Awakening. Harkening back to revivalist preaching and "harvests" (mass conversions) in the late seventeenth century, its most successful proponents, including the Reverends Gilbert Tennant (Presbyterian), George Whitefield (Anglican), and Jonathan Edwards (Congregationalist), adopted highly emotional, charismatic styles of preaching and emphasized the importance of having a conversion experience—what

Whitefield called "New Birth," referring to Jesus's declaration that "you must be born again."

In some respects the Great Awakening was the first American ecumenical movement. In order to work together to promote revivalism, several Christian denominations tabled their differences, which were rooted in ethnic identities as much as in doctrine or church governance. In fact, the channels of communication opened during this period would prove crucial to the success of the American Revolution decades later.

At the same time, the Great Awakening forced a split within American Protestantism between the progressive New Lights, who embraced revivalism, and the conservative Old Lights, who did not. Note that, in this context, the "liberal" forces of change were identified with evangelical revivalism, which emphasized spiritual experience and challenged established institutions of Christian religion.

Almost as quickly as it swept in, the revivalist spirit was swept away. By the mid-1740s, critics of the movement had gained the upper hand. Ministers such as Charles Chauncy in Boston argued that Christian conversion should be grounded in reason and careful thought rather than in emotional experience. As this view took hold, revivalist preachers lost ground. But the new spirit that these revivals had awakened would not disappear forever. In the aftermath, beneath the ashes, the embers glowed red.

Less than a century later, a Second Great Awakening took hold of and shook the spirit of the young United States, from Kentucky and the frontier South to New York and New England.

The first revival of the Second Great Awakening is remembered as the July 1800 revival at Creedence Clearwater Church in southwestern Kentucky. More significant, however, was the 1801 "camp meeting" at Cane Ridge in the forests of eastern Kentucky, so named because many people camped out for nearly a week of preaching, prayer, worship, singing, and dancing (the first Woodstock?). Led by a group of Baptist, Methodist, and Presbyterian ministers and attracting as many as 20,000 people, news of Cane Ridge spread quickly, sparking revivals throughout the country.

Other beginnings of the Second Great Awakening trace to a more austere reform movement at, of all places, Yale College. The instigator was Timothy Dwight, a pastor, theologian, and author whose grandfather on his mother's side was none other than Jonathan Edwards. On becoming the college's eighth president in 1795, Dwight initiated a series of reforms aimed at rooting out popular student interest in the "infidel philosophy" of Enlightenment thought identified with the French Revolution. In his 1797 address to the graduating class, "The Nature and Danger of Infidel Philosophy," he warned against the seduction of philosophies that are critical of Christian faith and Scriptural authority, fearing that even some of the young men in his audience would "fall prey":

> You will see one decent or doubtful person, and another, sliding slowly down the declivity of irreligion, and many more heedless, or more daring, leaping at once into the gulph beneath. Here, a companion will turn his back, and walk no more with Christ. There, a Parent, or Instructor, will forsake him, having loved the present world....Allured, awed, supported, perhaps without a friend at hand to pluck you by the arm, or to point to you either the danger or the means of escaping it, it can scarcely be hoped, that none of you will be destroyed. Most of the Infidels, whom I have known, have fallen a sacrifice to this cause, or to the fear of ridicule.

With reactionary exhortations and warnings such as this, Dwight's movement bore fruit among students, and many converted. As his disciples went out to take on leadership roles of their own, moreover, the movement carried well beyond the campus. The most notable among Dwight's disciples was Lyman Beecher, a great preacher and theologian whose work was formative for the development of evangelicalism.

Dwight's was a revival movement with a certain conservative, back-to-fundamentals flavor to it, concerned as it was with what he, as a good Calvinist, believed to be the natural human inclination to fall away from God's will and communion. Given Calvinism's strong emphasis on fallen human nature, it is only logical that Dwight would be dubious about the ability of human beings to choose what's right for them. In the age-old free will versus determinism debate, Calvinists come down strongly on the latter.

For Dwight, then, conversion and revival were understood be no more than divinely determined human responses to acts of divine grace. Although ecumenical, the first Great Awakening had nonetheless been rooted firmly in this Calvinist theology, understanding revival to be, as Dwight's grandfather Jonathan Edwards put it, "the surprising work of God," not of evangelists or converts. Dwight's call for revival was a call for devout and intellectual vigilance against the seductiveness of new ideas, believing that sinful nature makes people naturally susceptible to such evils. And he believed that any revival must be the work of divine providence and not a matter of human innovation or initiative.

Not so for other proponents of the Second Great Awakening. Although Dwight remained devoutly Calvinist in his understanding of sovereign grace and predestination, the Second Great Awakening that he helped initiate was dominated by another theological tradition, Arminianism, which was finding its way to the United States thanks especially to John Wesley, founder of the Methodist movement.

The Dutch theologian Jacob Arminius (1560–1609) had rejected certain tenets of what had become in his time orthodox Calvinism, most notably its doctrines of predestination and election, according to which there is nothing one can do to gain or lose salvation. For orthodox Calvinism, salvation is strictly a matter of God's sovereign grace. Free will is an illusion. Although Arminianism agrees that salvation is by grace alone, it also asserts that it is conditional on faith, so that one can, by God-given free will, resist God's grace and even lose salvation.

The implications of Arminian theology for revivalism are clear: people have free will to choose or resist salvation offered by God; and they may fall away; and they may return, repent, and be revived. The Second Great Awakening had theological roots in Dwight's Calvinist preaching, but it was this Arminian theology that came to dominate as it spread during the first three decades of the nineteenth century.

Enter the best-known revivalist of the Second Great Awakening, Charles Grandison Finney (1792–1875). In several influential books and sermons, he argued that revivals were not simply the "surprising work of God," but were effects of human effort and innovation aimed at exciting powerful emotions that would lead to repentance and obedience to God. His book, *Lectures on Revivals of Religion*, is a veritable how-to manual for doing revivals.

Almost all the religion in the world has been produced by revivals. God has found it necessary to take advantage of the excitability there is in mankind, to produce powerful excitements among them, before he can lead them to obey. Men are so sluggish, there are so many things to lead their minds off from religion, and to oppose the influence of the gospel, that it is necessary to raise an excitement among them, till the tide rises so high as to sweep away the opposing obstacles. They must be so excited that they will break over these counteracting influences, before they will obey God.

—Charles Grandison Finney, *Lectures on Revivals of Religion*, 1835

There were techniques, Finney argued, that open people's hearts and minds to repentance and return to God. Not that these "new measures," as he called them, would create such emotions or feelings. Rather, they are "calculated to excite them. . . . If you mean to break up the fallow ground of your hearts, you must begin by looking at your hearts—examine and note the state of your minds, and see where you are. Many never seem to think about this." Put this way, we can see a kind of Christian existentialism in Finney. His aim was not unlike Kierkegaard's, to strip an individual of all routines and habits of defense, to isolate that person from the crowd, and thereby to bring her or him alone before God in honest self-reflection.

One of Finney's most famous new measures was the "anxious bench," a front-row seat reserved for those in the congregation who felt the need to repent and return. Here they were set apart, literally, for intense introspection and for prayerful attention from the minister, family members, and friends.

As an evangelist, Finney's measures met with great success in revivals he held throughout western New York, which he described as a "hot bed" of spiritual reawakening. Others, more critical of the movement, would call it "burned-over." Some believe Finney's charismatic, extemporaneous preaching was responsible for as many as a half-million conversions.

Remember that in Arminian theology, one can lose one's salvation. Thus revivalist preachers emphasized sanctification, the idea that a Christian, once saved, must continue in a process of spiritual improvement toward greater and greater godliness through the work of the Holy Spirit. This theology led Finney and other preachers of the Second Great Awakening to emphasize moral reforms in society—most notably, the abolition of slavery. Finney and others (including Baptist and Methodist missionaries during roughly the same period) insisted that black slaves were equal to free whites in the eyes of God. All are created in God's image, they argued, and therefore slavery itself is an

7. Camp meeting, ca. 1829. Lithography by H. Bridport. In the wake of the famous 1801 revival at Cane Ridge, Kentucky, the camp meeting phenomenon spread throughout the country, drawing many thousands into the woods, sometimes for days at a time.

abomination against God's intentions for humankind. Finney often preached against slavery and even refused to serve Holy Communion to members of his congregation who owned slaves. As professor of theology and later (1852) president of Oberlin College, he continued to be a leader in the abolition movement.

But Finney was not the first white preacher to reach out to African Americans. As early as the 1770s, itinerant Methodist and Baptist preachers, also armed with an Arminian theological commitment to moral reform, evangelized slaves, often bringing them to membership in local congregations. Some racially mixed congregations even had African American ministers, and there were several well-known African American revivalist preachers, including women.

In many other cases, however, racist practices of segregation within congregations (including being refused Communion and being relegated to balcony spaces) led African Americans eventually to part ways and start their own denominations, such as the African Methodist Episcopal Church, established in 1815 under the leadership of Richard Allen (1760–1831). Nonetheless, it is clear that African American Christianity in America has deep roots in the revivalism of the late eighteenth and early nineteenth centuries.

Pentecosts

By the mid-nineteenth century, the nationwide consuming fire of the Second Great Awakening had slowed and cooled, some would say because there was nothing more to burn. But the cinders remained, and indeed the fires have rekindled again and again throughout American religious history: from the holiness revivals at camp meetings in Kentucky, Tennessee, North Carolina, and Georgia in the late 1800s, sparked by the charismatic preaching of Benjamin Harding Irwin and A. J. Tomlinson (founder of the Church of God tradition), to the more familiar, recent revival meetings of preachers like Billy Graham and Christian musicians like Keith Green.

One of the most significant of these descendent revival movements is Pentecostalism, which traces its beginnings to an interracial congregation meeting in Los Angeles, California, in 1906. Its leader was a charismatic African American preacher named William J. Seymour. Seymour was a disciple of revivalist preacher Charles Fox Parham, who taught that *glossolalia*, or the spiritual gift of speaking in tongues, was the defining mark of one's baptism by the Holy Spirit.

On April 9, 1906, Seymour's small congregation was overcome by a mass outbreak of tongues. It was a new Pentecost of sorts, much like that remembered in the second chapter of the New Testament book of the Acts of the Apostles. As news spread, Seymour's group grew rapidly. Soon they needed a

8. Early leaders of the Azusa Street Mission, 1907. Included here are the movement's leader, William J. Seymour (*front row, second from right*), and his wife, Mrs. Jenny Seymour (*back row, third from left*).

bigger space, so they moved to a house located at 312 Azusa Street. Thus the name, "the Azusa Street Revival."

The Pentecostal Apostolic Faith Movement, as Seymour called it, thrived on Azusa Street for three years before internal and external pressures began to break it apart. By then, however, many other Pentecostal preachers, black and white, women and men, were helping to spread the movement throughout the United States and around the world.

In Los Angeles, the most significant successor to Seymour was the very remarkable preacher and religious entrepreneur Aimee Semple McPherson (1890–1944). After years as a Salvation Army missionary in Hong Kong and revival preacher in Ontario and Rhode Island, she arrived in Los Angeles in 1918 in her "Gospel Auto," a black Oldsmobile with the message, "JESUS IS COMING SOON—GET READY," painted across its doors in large, white, capital letters. One night, she recounts, she heard a message from God: "Shout, for the Lord hath given you the city." Soon she was preaching to hundreds every day in rented halls. In 1922 she established the first radio station owned by a religious organization and was the first woman ever to preach on the radio. By 1923 she was preaching several times weekly at her $1.5 million, 5,000-seat Angelus Temple, which became the headquarters for her International Church of the Foursquare Gospel (incorporated in 1927).

McPherson's sermons were famous for vaudevillian flair, involving elaborate illustrations and dramatic staging. Once, dressed as a police officer, she rode up to her pulpit on a motorcycle.

By the time of McPherson's death in 1944, probably from a drug overdose after a revival meeting, the Foursquare church had close to 400 branches in North America, 200 foreign missions, and a

9. "Sister Aimee" Semple McPherson (1890–1944), founding minister of the International Church of the Foursquare Gospel in Los Angeles. Her spectacular "illustrated sermons" often rivaled anything Hollywood had to offer.

Bible college. Her son succeeded her as leader of the movement, which to this day continues to thrive and spread all over world.

Since the Azusa Street phenomenon about a century ago, America and the world have witnessed the tremendous growth in Pentecostalism (which includes the International Church of the Foursquare Gospel, Assemblies of God, the Church of God denominations, and many other charismatic and holiness churches). According to the *Yearbook of American and Canadian Churches*, membership in the Church of God in Christ, which is a predominantly African American Pentecostal denomination, grew from 200,470 in 1935 to 5,499,875 in 1991. The Assemblies of God denomination grew from 50,386 in 1925 to 2,830,861 in 2005, and is one of the fastest growing denominations today. The Assemblies of God church is consistently ranked as one of the fastest growing churches in America (along with the Catholic Church and the Church of Jesus Christ of Latter-day Saints). All three of these denominations are among the twenty-five largest Christian bodies in the United States today. Many smaller Pentecostal denominations demonstrate similarly dramatic growth.

From the margins

Although revivalist movements in America have tended to have a broad, inclusive, ecumenical spirit, we must not forget that they have also been controversial, often viewed as a threat to mainstream, established religious traditions and institutions. Indeed, they have often been condemned by the establishment as downright horrific and monstrous. Frances Trollope, for example, an upper-class English tourist in the United States, described her visit to a camp meeting in the wilds of Indiana in the early 1830s as a living nightmare, "an indescribable confusion of heads and legs . . . howlings and groans so terrible that I shall never cease to shudder when I recall them." She was

> Breathing strange utterances and mouthing a creed which it
> would seem no sane mortal could understand, the newest
> religious sect has started in Los Angeles. Meetings are held in a
> tumble-down shack on Azusa Street near San Pedro, and
> devotees of the weird doctrine practice the most fanatical rites,
> preach the wildest theories, and work themselves into a state of
> mad excitement in their peculiar zeal. Colored people and a
> sprinkling of whites compose the congregation, and night is
> made hideous in the neighborhood by the howlings of the
> worshippers who spend hours swaying back and forth in nerve-
> racking attitude of prayer and supplication. They claim to have
> the gift of tongues and to be able to comprehend the babble.
>
> —*Los Angeles Times* report on the Azusa Street Revivals, 1906 (quoted by Luis Lugo)

especially disturbed, tellingly enough, by the loud and unreserved
expressions of religious ecstasy from women. Such Bacchanal
behavior clearly offended her as improper and threatening to
established gender roles.

Nearly a century later, in 1906, the *Los Angeles Daily Times*
described the Azusa Street revival in similar terms of horror: filled
with "strange utterances...no sane mortal could understand...
night is made hideous in the neighborhood by the howlings of the
worshippers."

These and many other reports describe charismatic revivals as
wild orgies of pandemonium, representing the participants
themselves as insane, inhuman, monstrous. From the
perspective of mainstream society, standing outside the collective
experience, these revivals appear as a dangerous threat to the
order of things, an invasion of social chaos that undermines the
well established structures of authority within the home, the
church, and society as a whole.

For good reason. Revival movements have often been socially subversive of the status quo. They have often messed with hierarchies of power and access and with the boundaries between insiders and outsiders. Remember that it was in the context of revivals in the late eighteenth and early nineteenth centuries that African Americans were first welcomed into mainstream religious communities. Here also were the beginnings of the abolitionist movement. And these same revivals became a locus of religious and spiritual power for many women whose silence had been enforced in mainstream churches of the day. Finney, for example, was criticized severely for allowing women to speak, pray, and emote openly in his revival meetings. Indeed, as was powerfully demonstrated in the early rise of Pentecostalism with the Azusa Street revival and Aimee Semple McPherson's Foursquare movement, the communities that formed around such spirited revivals were often diverse, including women and men of different races and classes, any of whom might hold the pulpit and speak with authority as they felt led by the spirit. Who would dare object to the calling of the spirit, which blows where it will?

Revivalism and the evangelical consciousness

Each new revivalist movement is unique, of course. And yet none is imaginable without the birth of the uniquely American evangelical consciousness that took hold during the Second Great Awakening and that continues to this day. To be sure, that consciousness is itself multifaceted and complex, resisting any simple definition. Yet we may identify four hallmarks that appear in nearly all its manifestations.

First, theologically, it is rooted in the Arminian tradition of Protestant Christianity. Rejecting a strict Calvinist doctrine of predestination, it sees *salvation* as something that can be gained, lost, and regained. Salvation is not a fact but an ongoing process of sanctification by which one grows more and more Christlike in one's daily moral and devotional life. Or not. Thus the need for revival and rededication.

Second, and again in reaction to traditional Calvinism, this American evangelical consciousness places a premium on *religious experience* and powerful emotions. We saw this in Finney's writings about the need to excite feelings through preaching and other "new measures." Wesleyans likewise valued the experience of a "warm heart" far more than whatever joys some orthodox Presbyterians might get from the rigor of systematic theology and a proper order of worship. (Disapproving of the wild emotionalism of revival camp meetings, the 1805 General Assembly of the Presbyterian Church declared, "God is a God of order and not of confusion, and whatever tends to destroy the comely order of his worship is not from him.")

The third hallmark follows from the first two. If salvation can be gained and lost, and if emotions are key to awakening the desire for conversion and rededication, then *revivalism* is necessarily a human activity and not simply "the surprising work of God." A successful revival, that is, a revival that draws many people and produces many converts, requires its preachers and organizers to deploy certain techniques that "produce powerful excitements." Revivals are staged, scripted, and performed.

The fourth and final hallmark of the American evangelical consciousness follows from the third. Given that revival depends on human techniques aimed at arousing intense religious feeling, it's no surprise that this consciousness is oriented toward *charismatic individual leaders*. Revivals occur around exciting preachers who have mastered tried and true techniques or who have developed their own special new measures. Think of Finney, McPherson, and Graham. At the center of a successful revival is a compelling personality.

So prevalent are these features within so many varieties of evangelical and charismatic Christianity today that one might think they were as old as the Apostle Paul himself. Many Christians would argue that they in fact are. And many of those would go so far as to say that you can't be a true Christian without embracing them, in spite of the fact that most Christians in the world don't. The fact that these hallmarks of evangelical consciousness have become so closely identified with the essential tenets of Christianity in the United States today is evidence of the powerful influence of revivalism in American religious history.

Roots of the American paradox

Having delved into the histories of possession and dispossession, the struggle for religious freedom, and revivalism, we may ask, what light—and what shadows—does this historical perspective cast on that uniquely American paradox of the *pluribus* and the *unum*, the many and the one?

On the one hand, we can see very clearly how the religious individualism of maverick, "outsider" religious persons and groups finds historical roots in the struggle for religious freedom, which placed a premium on the right of a person to think and act according to her or his own conscience, as she or he feels religiously led, even in dissent from the majority. It also finds roots in the history of revivalism, which raised the value of individual religious experience and feeling. Thus, for example, we often see new religious movements beginning with a single person's claim to have had a new religious experience or divine revelation. In the eyes of many Americans, such a personal experience is enough to legitimate a new religion.

On the other hand, we have gained some historical perspective on the drive toward religious unity and conformity in American society, especially as that drive has been expressed in the powerful influence of evangelical Protestant Christian beliefs and moral values through the rise of the Christian Right. Most obviously, this movement bears several key marks of the American evangelical consciousness born of the history of revivalism. At its center are charismatic preachers skilled at mobilizing people by stirring their emotions with religious fervor. The theological orientation is essentially Arminian, seeing salvation and divine favor—for individuals and for the nation—as things that can be lost, therefore requiring repentance and return. Like the revivalists of the Second Great Awakening, the movement is eager to engage in political activism to legislate moral reforms in society. And at its heart is an ecumenical spirit that overlooks denominational differences of doctrine in order to build a larger movement with a shared identity centered on social reform.

At the same time, in its drive to establish a conservative Christian, moralistic *unum* in the United States, it undermines religious freedom and the separation of church and state. It envisions a Christian nation whose Manifest Destiny does not leave room for religious differences, especially when those differences are incompatible with its political platform.

Today, in fact, the Christian Right's *moral* agenda delineates the extent of its ecumenism far more clearly than any point of theology. It is more comfortable partnering with morally conservative Mormons, whose faith its leaders denounce as a "cult" but who oppose abortion and gay rights, than with progressive or liberal Protestants who support these things—even on Christian biblical-theological grounds. Major doctrinal differences are not necessarily deal breakers; disagreements with its social and moral platform are.

Chapter 4
Looking Ahead
Forces of Change

Let's consider some very recent forces of change. We can think of them as three risings: the rise of religious diversity in America, the rise of the information society, and the rise of consumer culture.

I'm not sure if everything that rises must converge. I take Flannery O'Connor's pronouncement that they must as a declaration of faith. But certainly these three risings are converging. Taken separately their influence on the religious landscape of America would be great enough; taken together their influence will be exponentially greater, radically changing that landscape forever.

The rise of religious diversity

One of the most striking features of America's religious landscape today is its remarkable diversity. It's fair to say that religious diversity in America today is both quantitatively and qualitatively greater than anywhere else in the world.

Of course, America has always been religiously diverse. Even in the eighteenth century, a wide range of religious traditions were represented, including several different Protestantisms linked to different ethnic origins (Dutch Presbyterians, British Anglicans, etc.), French and Spanish Catholics (and before them, Spanish Muslims), Jews, various new religious movements, indigenous religions of Native American peoples, and the African tribal religions of slaves. By the nineteenth century, Muslims from the Middle East and Confucians and Buddhists from East Asia were also being added to the mix. Nonetheless, as we have seen, the early United States were dominated, culturally and governmentally, by a strong majority identified with Christianity, especially Protestant Christianity. It was, in many significant respects, a Christian country.

In recent decades, however, we have seen the floodgates of religious diversity swing open. Unprecedented religious diversity is already a fact and is bound to rise in the coming decades.

How has it come to this? How, as Diana L. Eck so aptly puts it, has an essentially Christian country become the most religiously diverse nation in the world, past or present?

The story is complex, of course, but Eck is right to point out one especially significant piece of legislation: the Immigration and Nationality Act of 1965, initiated by President Kennedy and signed into law by President Johnson. Like the Civil Rights Act of 1964,

> The religious landscape of America has changed radically in the past thirty years, but most of us have not yet begun to see the dimensions and scope of that change, so gradual has it been and yet so colossal.... This is an astonishing new reality. We have never been here before.
>
> —Diana L. Eck, *A New Religious America: How a "Christian Country" Has Become the World's Most Religiously Diverse Nation*

it sought to address directly the long and tragic history of institutional racism in the United States. Since 1924, people from the so-called Asia–Pacific triangle had been barred from immigration, and immigration quotas were linked to "original" populations of the country. There was a growing understanding that these immigration laws were foundational to the structures of racism in the United States and therefore needed to be dismantled. Of course, self-interest was also a factor: the Cold War, the space race, and other global competitions motivated efforts to attract the "best and the brightest," whatever their homeland, to carry out scientific research and development in the national interest.

Since this act passed, sources of immigration to the United States have shifted from Europe to other parts of the world, especially Asia, and this shift has led in turn to a tremendous, historically unprecedented growth of religious diversity in America. United States Census data bears out the dramatic population shifts that have come in its wake:

* The percentage of Americans who are foreign born has doubled since 1990, to more than 10 percent.

* In the last decade of the twentieth century, the Asian population in the United States grew by 43 percent to nearly 10.8 million.

* Between 1990 and 2000, the Hispanic population grew by 38.8 percent to more than 31.3 million.

* Projections for 2010 indicate an additional growth in the Asian population of roughly 24 percent to 14.2 million, and an additional growth in the Hispanic population of 34 percent to 47.8 million. These numbers far outpace the population growth projections for "whites."

Remember that U.S. Census data does not identify the religious affiliations of these ethnic groups. Nonetheless, it is beyond dispute that religious diversity (including diversities of Christianity) in the

United States is rising along with the rising numbers of the ethnic groups represented by these new populations.

Over the past decade, Eck and the Pluralism Project have made the compelling case to move beyond mere *tolerance* of this new and ever-rising religious diversity in order to build a pluralistic social movement that proactively embraces religious differences in order to enrich American society.

Of course, there are also social movements pushing in the opposite direction. Largely ignorant of non-Christian religious traditions and fearful of the ways this new and growing religious diversity will continue to transform our landscape, these movements want to dismantle the liberal immigration legislation of 1965 and fortify a Christian identity for the nation, however nostalgic or mythical its origins may be. Indeed, it is no accident that the rise of the Christian Right had its beginnings in the 1970s as a reaction to the liberal legislations from the previous decade. The rising religious diversity of America inspires rising hopes *and* rising fears.

The rise of the information society

Information age ... information revolution ... knowledge economy ... intangible economy ... network society. ... These and similar terms are all circling around a revolution still very much in progress. Simultaneously global and local, technical and social, there is no nook of human existence that will escape its consequences. Needless to say, it has everything to do with the future of religion in America.

This revolution has emerged from the convergence of three initially independent inventions in the 1980s. First, the popularization of compact, affordable **Personal Computers** with their own microprocessors and common software platforms, initially popularized by Apple and then promoted in an open-standard form by IBM, made it easy for people to share documents, software, and other media on a common platform. Second, **digitization** brought together widely varied analog media (texts, sounds, still images, videos) into a common digital format based on a binary code of zeros and ones. Although digital innovations in music, film, and computers were initially independent of one another, they soon converged, enabling people to share visual, audio, and textual media in a common, easily interchangeable form and, perhaps more significantly, to create new works that incorporate older media within them (e.g., "sampling"). Third, with the popularization of the personal computer and digitization, new communication technologies developed in order to connect computers to one another and to larger remote servers. Behold the **World Wide Web**, a global, potentially limitless hypertextual network that runs on the Internet, invented around 1990 by Tim Berners-Lee.

Together these three innovations constitute a revolution that is not simply technological but sociological, radically transforming the way we understand our world and relate to one another, on every scale from the most local to the most global.

Some describe ours as a knowledge economy, driven by what Manuel Castells calls "informationalism." Insofar as information is understood as the communication of knowledge, every society is an information society. But information*alism* is something categorically different, a "*form of social organization* in which information generation, processing, and transmission become the

> The growing integration between minds and machines ... [is] fundamentally altering the way we are born, we live, we learn, we work, we produce, we consume, we dream, we fight, or we die.
>
> —Manuel Castells, *The Rise of the Network Society*

fundamental sources of productivity and power." Here information is the primary object of exchange. New technologies are not the means of producing and distributing whatever things are determined to be good; rather, new technologies aim at ever more efficient accumulation and processing of information. Castells writes,

> What characterizes the current technological revolution is not the centrality of knowledge and information, but the application of such knowledge and information to knowledge generation and information processing/communication devices, in a cumulative feedback loop between innovation and the uses of innovation.... Thus computers, communication systems, and genetic decoding and programming are all *amplifiers and extensions of the human mind.* (emphasis added)

As are, potentially, all the other minds that are communicating with one another within this network society.

Such revolutionary changes are bringing out the utopians and the doomsayers among us. I suggest we avoid such extremes. There's good news here, to be sure, but there's also bad news, and the two are often linked. Let me highlight three "good news, bad news" implications of the information society that are particularly significant for religion in America. Each has to do with the tension between democratization and control.

On the one hand (the good news), the information revolution bears a certain democratizing spirit. It empowers individuals and groups to achieve greater knowledge through greater access to more information. There is an overwhelming amount of information on the Internet about various religious traditions, practices, ideas, and institutions. Many specific religious communities, moreover, are making information about themselves available on the Web. Today there is more information for Americans about religion, religions, and religious communities, and more opportunity for religious groups to inform the larger public about themselves, than ever before.

On the other hand (the bad news), the rise of the network society can be seen as a new organization of social power, with winners and losers, franchised and disenfranchised. Access is far from an equal opportunity, even in the United States. The information society is not a democratic, level playing field of equal access. This is plainly evident in the fact that different people, businesses, and households have better or worse machines and faster or slower connections. Beyond that, a great many do not have a connection at all. At the time of this writing, 29 percent of American households (31 million homes) do not have Internet access and are not planning to get it. And then there are America's poor, homeless, and otherwise dispossessed, nearly invisible in the urban and rural landscapes of industrial society, banished to utter oblivion in the rising information society. There is a fourth world of Americans who are not on the Internet or in the network and therefore, according to the ontology of the network society, virtually nonexistent.

Beyond access to information, moreover, there is the matter of control. Who is gathering, storing, processing, generating, and distributing the information that we might want to access? In industrial society, power was concentrated in what Castells calls "spaces of places," that is, physical places of production and distribution. In the network society, power is concentrated less in the "spaces of places" than in the "spaces of flows" of information. Such spaces link together distant locations around shared interests concerning the processing of information. Spaces of flows have three "layers": the material infrastructure, that is, the electronic circuits and devices that make networking possible; nodes and hubs of control and exchange that organize the circuits into networks and manage the flow of information; and the elites who manage the direction and functions of flows of information within these networks. These managerial elites are the new upper class. They are the managers of information at the heart of the spaces of flows, where, as Castells puts it, "make-believe is belief in the making." In this light, the belief that the information age is empowering the masses by making information and communication more readily accessible begins to appear more than a little naïve.

How about individual freedom? On the one hand (the good news), the rise of the information society bears with it a sense of individual empowerment to pursue knowledge and connection within a free market of information. It seems to get us out from under the authority of those who want to control what we read or watch and with whom we communicate. It opens up much greater freedom of choice. It provides outlets of communication and information that run counter to the dominant, authoritative voices within any particular social context.

Think, for example, of the many blogs by reporters, citizens, and American military personnel in Iraq and Afghanistan, often offering perspectives that are quite different from those presented in Pentagon press conferences.

Looking Ahead

Think of how difficult it has become for governments to control whether individuals read or see (and share) certain prohibited texts or images (assassinations, executions, and massacres, for example).

Think of a teenager growing up in a religiously restrictive home or community, who is able to pursue taboo questions about her own or other religions via the Internet. The network society has no center, no single control point, and therefore offers individuals multiple means of bypassing the will of central authorities.

On the other hand (the bad news), freedom is always under surveillance. Everything we do on the Internet and other networking devices is data. Google, for example, stores every search that it runs and every link that is clicked from its results. If you have registered with Google, then those searches may be linked to you specifically. Internet Service Providers (ISPs) also have the capability to collect data on the activities of their users (email, Web browsing), and often do. Why? Because everything we do is information. We are information sources. We *are* information. Storage of our digital activities is relatively cheap, and who knows when some bit of information might turn out to be valuable? It is far from clear, moreover, what kind of constraints businesses and governments have on accessing that information. Internet privacy does not really exist, and what is freedom without privacy? The feeling of freedom and autonomy while "surfing the Net" is, again, naïve.

Finally, on the one hand (the good news), the rising information society empowers people and groups to form their own, networked social identities, including religious identities. The Web and other networking and communication technologies (international call-in radio shows, like the BBC's *World Have Your Say*) enable people to form relationships with like-minded and like-spirited people all over the world and to create "virtual" communities with them.

Often, these new social identities incorporate hybrid mixtures of various distinct religious traditions. In the music world, the digital revolution has led to the creation of "mashups," songs that incorporate more or less recognizable elements from other songs. A simple example, using only two sources, is Pink's "Get the Party Started" voice track mashed with The Clash's "Rock the Casbah." An artist like Girl Talk (aka Greg Gillis) offers far more complex works, sampling hundreds of different artists' tracks into his own albums. The result is creative work that is entirely derivative and entirely new.

We find a similar creative dynamic emerging in the networked worlds of religious identity. "Religious mashups," let's call them. Such things were practically impossible before the invention of global, digital networking, which is not only about getting and using information but also about connecting people and media in ways that have never been possible before.

Within the spaces of flows in the network society, new conceptions of religious identity and community are emerging. They rely less on traditional Western notions of subjectivity, which emphasize autonomy and integrity—the idea of the individual as an autonomous, free actor whose various aspects of identity all come together into an integrated whole person. In the world of the Net, social identity is virtual, created through connections in networks. Identity becomes a set of specific connections, a little network, a small net holding a group of elements, or people, together within the ever-expanding World Wide Web.

On the other hand (the bad news), such a networked sense of identity, located in the spaces of flows rather than in the spaces of places, can, paradoxically, lead to individual isolation and social fragmentation. As social groups are alienated from each other in physical proximity and everyday, face-to-face communication, Castells observes, they are more likely to "see the other as a stranger, eventually as a threat. In this process, social fragmentation spreads, as identities become more specific and increasingly difficult to share. The information society, in its global manifestation, is also the world of Aum Shinrikyo, of the American militia, of Islamic/Christian theocratic ambitions." It is no coincidence that these are all religious groups.

The rise of consumer culture

"I shop, therefore I am." I used to see this post-Cartesian proof of existence on a lot of bumpers. I don't see it as much these days. Why? Maybe because by now it goes without saying. Thinking is all well and good, but consuming has become, in mainstream America, a more widely trusted mark of what it means to be fully human. Shopping is no longer "retail therapy": it is the meaning of life.

There was a time when religion seemed to be set apart from consumer culture. Our word sacred (Latin *sacer*) means, most basically, "set apart," unscathed by the mainstream, everyday, profane world of mundane existence. So seemed religion, that protector of sacred things, in relation to the marketplace. It seemed to be set apart, unscathed by those capitalist forces that were putting a price on everything else worth having or being. Perhaps it was inevitable in our world that the sacred, too, in whatever form it takes in time and space, would either be given market value or be banished to the realm of cultural oblivion. In our society, the existence of things that cannot be bought or sold is increasingly suspect.

Not that religion's marriage to capitalism is entirely new. Indeed, as several historians of religion in America have shown, the rise of capitalism drew a good deal of inspiration from evangelical Protestantism, and vice versa. Most of the men responsible for the tremendous missionary success of the American Bible Society and Gideons International in the early nineteenth century, for example, were not ministers but entrepreneurs, who applied their business models of efficiency and organization to their efforts to publish and distribute Bibles.

> Since my daughter was two years old, she has been intrigued with our Nativity set.... She was interested in the stories that went with the figures: Jesus, Mary, Joseph, the shepherds, the animals, the Magi positioned still at a distance... just as she was interested in the stories that went with more brightly colored figures a few feet away: a pink baby pig, a blue donkey, a honey colored bear, and a young boy named Christopher Robin.... We are certainly incited to choose, but choices are not exclusive. Choose and choose again. Jesus, Pooh and the Lion King as well. *Gloria in Excelsis Deo! Hakuna Matata!*
>
> —Vincent J. Miller, *Consuming Religion*

Likewise, the revivalists of the Second Great Awakening were not averse to using marketing techniques to attract masses. And Aimee Semple McPherson, famous for her vaudevillian sermon-performances, was very well aware that she was competing with the burgeoning Los Angeles entertainment industry for an audience. More recently, evangelical promoters of "church growth" are urging churches to treat members and potential members as customers. Suffice to say, "church shopping" is by now a dead metaphor.

Of course, there is always a degree of ambivalence among evangelical Christians about the movement's close relationship with consumer culture, especially its marketing approach to "spreading the Word." At the heart of this ambivalence are two imperatives that often conflict: to get the Gospel message out by whatever means necessary, and to preserve the sanctity of its scriptures and traditions. In the evangelical Christian publishing industry, for example, one often hears expressions of unease about going too far and, in the process, diluting the sanctity and integrity of its Christian mission. For the most part, however, it has sallied forth, to the extent that it's often hard to distinguish evangelism from marketing.

Looking Ahead

Although evangelicals were early adopters of consumer models, other religious traditions have proven to be at least as marketable. This is especially true for those traditions rich in things, that is, ritual objects and images. All the more so if those things seem exotic to most mainstream American consumers. If you don't agree, just browse through your nearby Pier 1 Imports or World Market and count the Buddhas, Shivas, Ganeshas, Confuciuses, prayer rugs, Blessed Virgin Marys, Saint Francises, ghost catchers, prayer beads, labyrinths, and crosses (crucifixes? not so much, interestingly). And watch for them on television, especially in shows about communicating with the dead, and in movie theaters, especially in supernatural horror films. Religion is selling. And so long as that's true, rumors of its death will be greatly exaggerated.

Religion is culture.

I understand that many will argue the opposite: that insofar as my depiction of religion's incorporation by the culture industry is accurate, religion is dead; that "true religion" is by definition *set apart* from our mainstream consumer culture; that true religion can never sell out.

As a religious person who gets goose bumps when reading the radical, countercultural prophetic voices of an Amos or a Dorothy Day, I am sympathetic to this viewpoint. I've preached it and taught it in Sunday school.

But as a scholar of religion, I understand that religion is inseparable from culture. Indeed, religion *is* culture. To think that religion in America is only "true" or "authentic" when it is pure and unadulterated by the consumer culture that is its larger context is not only idealistic but, again, naïve.

Religion in America today is part and parcel of the culture industry. It is a cultural reservoir, a deep mine of symbolic ideas and objects that can be excavated, refined, reproduced, and sold to people who are seeking, through consumption, to build meaningful lives. Religion is commodity.

This is not to say that people within our capitalist society are strictly passive consumers, spoon-fed mass-produced goods, religious and otherwise, by a culture industry that's calling all the shots. There are creative dimensions to consumerism, as consumers make choices about what kinds of popular culture they embrace and how they combine different elements of it into specific cultural identities for themselves.

Indeed, with the rise of consumer culture, we are witnessing the rise of a kind of consumer mentality with regard religious identity. As religious cultural products become more readily available for purchase, and as fewer and fewer Americans are raised with a strong sense of traditional religious affiliation, many are creating

Religion in America

their own ensembles or mashups of religious identity, often mixing and matching elements from different traditions to create more or less individual, hybrid combinations, most of which will change with the seasons and the arrival of new lines. While some are church shopping, others are religious identity shopping.

Inspired by the Marxist philosopher and cultural theorist Theodor Adorno, a growing number of scholars see consumer culture to be a kind of religion of the masses. Is the reverse also true? Is religion becoming, at least for some, a form of consumerism? Is religious consumerism the inevitable end of religion in this increasingly consumption-driven society?

Responses

It is really impossible to talk about any one of these three risings without talking about the other two. The growing religious diversity in America is amplified by the availability of religious information and the potential to form new religious identities in an increasingly networked society. Religious consumerism feeds voraciously on the rich diversity of religious identities and cultures that are now available in the physical and virtual spaces that Americans occupy. More and more religious ideas, images, and things—digital and material alike—from all over the world are ever more readily available to consumers, shopping for meaning, purpose, and identity in the marketplace of culture. At the same time, within this religiously diverse, consumerist, networked society, the possibilities for creating, even "mashing up," religious identities from the wealth of religious cultures available to them, and the possibilities for building religious communities around those identities, are radically different from the possibilities afforded by earlier industrial and pre-industrial societies.

Still, not all religion in America today, or tomorrow, is simply conforming itself to these emerging and converging forces of social change. In fact, we often see religious social movements taking form *over against* one or more of these forces, even while they embrace the others. Consider, for example, the rise of the Christian Right since the late 1970s. It has been especially savvy in promoting itself in the media of our new information society. Indeed, one of its main proponents, Pat Robertson, was a media mogul long before he got into politics, and his highly influential Christian Coalition owes much of its success to its savvy use of the Internet and its understanding of how traditional television, radio, and print news media are changing. This movement has also worked successfully within consumer culture, to which traditional news media outlets must cater in the emerging "marketplace of ideas." Yet, even as it has taken advantage of the rise of consumerism and the information society, it has defined itself in reaction against the liberal culture and policies of the 1960s, which, as we saw, opened American society to greater religious diversity.

On the other hand, old-school liberal Christians such as the Quakers have reacted strongly against the rise of consumer culture but have embraced and promoted religious pluralism through interreligious dialogue on matters of social justice and human rights. And some sectarian groups have virtually dropped off the network, refused to participate in consumer culture, and separated themselves from exposure to people with different religious identities. Still other, radical, even militant religious movements sometimes use these emerging forces in order to undermine them. Consider, for example, Al Qaeda or the Aryan Nations, who share information and form "phantom cells" within the very same network society that they proclaim to be the virtual embodiment of evil in the world.

Love them or hate them, use them or refuse them, there is no escaping the influence of these converging forces. They are already radically transforming the American religious landscape, and they will continue to do so, in ways that remain largely unimaginable.

Chapter 5

To Coin a Phrase

E Pluribus Unum As Ideal and Dilemma

In the footsteps of Tocqueville

Wartime boycotts of French fries and French toast notwithstanding, Americans have always been anxious to know what non-Americans, especially Europeans, even more especially the French, think of us and our society. Ever hopeful for a paternal word or smile of approval, our boisterous defensiveness in response to criticisms only reveals a shadow side of insecurity within a nation that still, in some very profound ways, feels like a younger prodigal sibling struggling to make good.

Our uneasy fascination with how Europeans see America is perhaps most evident in the abiding authority of Alexis de Tocqueville, the French philosopher, lawyer, and aristocrat who, at the age of twenty-five, spent nine months of 1831 touring the eastern United States and southeastern Canada on the King of France's dime with his colleague Gustave de Beaumont. His two-volume sociological travel narrative based on that tour, *Democracy in America* (1835 and 1840), remains one of the most quoted commentaries on America to this day. Politicians of all stripes; from Bill Clinton to Newt Gingrich, cite it with reverence, as though it were sacred scripture. Many read it like an old, yellowing report card from kindergarten days that, while pointing out some minor problems and potential pitfalls, was generally very positive, revealing a certain inspired and inspiring idealism at the heart of the American democratic experiment that heralded a new chapter in the history of human progress toward enlightenment and liberty.

Tocqueville described American society as "a thousand different elements recently assembled...up to the present one cannot say that there is an American character, at least unless it is the very fact of not having any." Having "no common memory, no national attachments here," he wondered what held this country together. What gave it coherence and identity?

A big part of the answer, he came to believe, was religion. But how could that be? How was it that religion was more influential in this nation, whose government was expressly separated from church authority, than it was in European nations, whose governments were overtly religious? He came to conclude that religion's greater

A countless number of sects in the United States all have differing forms of worship they offer to the Creator but they all agree about the duties that men owe to each other.... Moreover, all the sects in the United States unite in the body of Christendom whose morality is everywhere the same.... It cannot, therefore, be said that religion exercises any influence on the laws and on the details of political opinions in the United States but it does control behavior and strives to regulate the state by regulating the family.... In the United States, religion governs not only behavior but extends its influence to men's minds.

—Alexis de Tocqueville, *Democracy in America*, 1835

social influence in America was precisely *because* of that separation. In contrast to France and other European nations, where the church was closely allied with the state, religious influence in the United States was largely *indirect*, based on what he described as a commonly shared Christian *moral* orientation, independent of the doctrinal differences among the "countless" sects that thrived there. This common morality did not impinge directly on freedom itself; rather, he wrote, it "effectively instructs Americans on *how* to be free" (emphasis added).

Remember that Tocqueville's 1831 visit coincided with the peak of the Second Great Awakening, a time when Christian leaders of all stripes were calling on Americans to set aside doctrinal differences in order to pursue a more universal evangelical revival of faith and piety, and to work together to provide moral leadership in addressing larger social-political issues such as slavery. Tocqueville was wrong, we know, to assert that all religious groups in America at that time were Christian, but it obviously seemed that way to him. In any case, the *pluribus* seemed to him to be finding their *unum* in a broadly shared, basically Christian code of moral behavior and values.

Still, Tocqueville worried about a "tyranny of the majority" that tended to marginalize or ostracize the individual, the particular, the countercultural that stood out from the crowd. In America, he observed, it is believed that there is greater intelligence in the greater number, and that the interests of the many take precedent over those of the few. This democratic ethos can generate a spirit of conformism and an aversion to individuals who think or act differently.

Often, as we well know, minority differences within American society are religiously marked. From witches to Jews to Jehovah's Witnesses to Native Americans to Shiite Muslims, the "foreign body" within the majority is very often represented in terms of religious difference. This is the dark side of religious unity, whether during the Second Great Awakening of the 1830s or during the rise of the Christian Right in the 1970s. Is the tyranny of the majority ever more foreboding than when it is expressing religious unity?

Recently, the *Atlantic Monthly* magazine invited a contemporary French philosopher and social commentator, Bernard-Henri Lévy, to make his own Tocquevillean tour of the United States. His very thoughtful and often insightful *American Vertigo: Traveling America in the Footsteps of Tocqueville* (2006) is the result.

Like his predecessor, Lévy is fascinated by this nation's lack of any solid grounding in a shared history, common ethnicity, or connection to a particular land. It is a "nation without foundation or substrate."

Lévy also shares Tocqueville's concern about the "tyranny of the majority." But he, like many others these days, is more concerned with "a risk of the tyranny of minorities." More than a century and a half after Tocqueville, Lévy does not find coherence in anything close to a shared commitment to a certain generic Christian moral orientation. Rather, he observes a kind of Balkanization of individual and collective identities, "the transformation of America into a plural nation, a mosaic of communities, a rhapsody of ethnic groups and collectivities that make increasingly problematic the realization of the venerable project . . . inscribed as the motto of the country: *E pluribus unum.*" Rich in *pluribus* but finding less and less *unum*, he believes that America faces an identity crisis.

Between Tocqueville and Lévy, we recognize the dilemma embedded in the great American ideal expressed so succinctly on the back of a penny. How to find unity and identity without erasing or ostracizing those who are different, other, difficult or impossible to integrate? How to lift up the plurality of individual differences without losing a shared sense of unity and identity? How can *unum* come from an ever changing and growing *pluribus*?

The challenge is huge. Indeed, it may be the greatest challenge American democracy will ever face. But we know where to begin. In today's op-ed world of provocative diatribe, where it sometimes seems that all ears and all channels are tuned to the loudest, most inhospitable, most polarizing, and most simplistic opinions about religion, where religious and antireligious fundamentalisms are all the rage, what we need above all is a commitment to the hard work of listening to and sharing beliefs, practices, and experiences about religion with the goal of understanding. By understanding, I simply mean recognizing how another's beliefs, practices, and experiences are personally meaningful. In this endeavor our motto might be from the Roman playwright Terence: "*Homo sum, humani nil a me alienum puto*," "I am human. Nothing human is foreign to me."

The stranger becomes the host

We began this very short introduction locally, exploring the *pluribus* of religion in my own urban neighborhood. Many would expect to find growing religious diversity in a big American city like Cleveland. But it's happening outside the cities too. By way of closing, let me share a story of America's changing religious landscape in a very different locale. It's about a Zen Buddhist temple and retreat center nestled in, of all places, eastern Kentucky's Daniel Boone National Forest. Famous as the homeland of the colonial frontiersman and Indian fighter Daniel Boone and as the hotbed of camp meeting revivals during the Second Great Awakening, these woods are now helping to host one of America's most recent popular religious movements, Zen Buddhism.

Like many American intellectuals in the 1960s and 1970s, Robert W. Genthner, now known as Zen Master Dae Gak, discovered Buddhism through the writings of Alan Watts, a one-time Episcopal priest and a gifted interpreter of East Asian thought within the Christian theological ethos. As a doctoral student in clinical psychology at Kent State and later as a professor of psychology at Eastern Kentucky University, Genthner continued to pursue Zen in

...est, eventually going under the tutelage of Korean Zen Master ...ung Sahn (who gave him permission to teach in 1988, and transmission, thereby becoming a Zen Master, in 1994).

In 1980 he and his then spouse Mara Genthner established a Zen center in the basement of their Lexington, Kentucky, home. In 1986, having outgrown that space, they scraped together $35,000 and purchased an old farm on Powell County's Furnace Mountain, named for two iron smelting furnaces that once provided the cannon balls for the Battle of New Orleans. Following Zen Master Seung Sahn's advice, based on principles of Korean and Chinese geomancy (outdoor Feng Shui), they built a temple, Kwan Se Um Sang Ji Sah ("Perceive World Sound High Ground Temple"), at the base of a massive cliff face on the mountain. More than two decades later, the center is thriving, with its temple, several log cabins, and a teahouse nestled into roughly 800 acres of rugged Kentucky wilderness. The site of many retreats and other events throughout the year, Furnace Mountain has become the center of a network of Zen communities guided by Zen Master Dae Gak's teaching, including ones in Ohio, Texas, Washington, DC, the UK, and Germany.

The wilderness has often been a locus of religious genesis. It was in the wilderness that Moses received the call to lead his people out of slavery. The Hebrews themselves wandered in the wilderness for forty years before entering the Promised Land. Jesus spent forty days in the wilderness before beginning his ministry. In biblical tradition, the wilderness is a primordial, chaotic place from which new things are born. It is a place of new beginnings. So too, often, in American religious history.

In fact, only forty miles north of Furnace Mountain is Cane Ridge, the site of the famous 1801 camp meeting that sparked the Second Great Awakening. Its gigantic log meeting house, which was built by Scottish Presbyterians who were instructed to settle there by Daniel Boone himself, still stands on that site and continues to be

used for worship. Furnace Mountain and Cane Ridge share t.
same wilderness beginnings.

Like those Cane Ridge revivalists two centuries ago, and like the
snake-handling Christians that have thrived in the mountains of
eastern Kentucky and Tennessee since the early twentieth century,
the Furnace Mountain community's reception by mainstream
Kentuckians has sometimes been less than warm. Zen Master Dae
Gak remembers discovering a local flyer that decried three great
evils that plague Powell County: the stabbing murders of a seven-
year-old girl and her mother by a fifteen-year-old boy in 1978; the
murders of a sheriff and deputy sheriff, shot in the back by a
wanted man in 1992; and the Zen Buddhist temple on Furnace
Mountain. Now and then a group of drunken rednecks will sling
slurs as they pass by. Occasionally the center has had visits from
less than sympathetic fundamentalist Christians who believe that
it is possessed by the Devil and aim to exorcise it.

Zen Master Dae Gak takes it all in with an appropriately Zenlike
sense of irony and humor. Noting that Furnace Mountain has a
reputation among townspeople as a lawless region of bootleggers
and other criminals, he suggests that his community fits into a
certain profile of "religious outlaws." In response to those who
pronounce them an evil presence in the region, he offers an
invitation: "We're open to anyone who wants to come here. And
hey, if they can get the Devil out of the place, *great*!" And he and his
Vice Abbot, Kosen Osho, fondly remember the elderly Christian
woman who was quoted in the local paper saying that she didn't
mind them being there, "as long as they use the King James
Version."

No doubt this warm, disarming demeanor also helps diffuse
potential conflicts. Zen Master Dae Gak tells the story of a
friendship he developed with a local Baptist preacher. On their
first meeting, the preacher asked him, "Have you ever walked
holding the hand of Jesus?"

thought for a moment and then responded, "I can't think of
me when I *haven't* walked holding the hand of Jesus." After that
nitial conversation, the preacher would sometimes come to pray
in the temple at Furnace Mountain—probably for the conversion
of Zen Master Dae Gak and his colleagues. In any case, he was
always welcomed, and over time he and Zen Master Dae Gak
developed a friendship in which they gradually came to understand
what each might mean by "walking holding the hand of Jesus."

"At Furnace Mountain we try moving in the world in a way of
inseparability, believing that we are more alike than different."
Within Zen Buddhist tradition, the movement toward hospitality
and inclusion of the seeming stranger comes from a mindfulness of
the fact that everything is connected and interdependent. To
exclude another person from community, or from the pale of
understandability, is as absurd as excluding one's own leg from
one's body.

Indeed, the community at Furnace Mountain has been very
intentional about reaching out to build goodwill and mutual
understanding. Zen Master Dae Gak frequently participates in
interreligious dialogues and has led retreats at the nearby Abbey of
Gethsemani, home of the late Trappist monk Thomas Merton, well
known for his interest, as a devout Catholic, in Zen Buddhism.
Furnace Mountain happily welcomes Christian church groups who
wish to hold their own retreats there and hosts annual visits from
high school students who are part of the state Governor's Scholars
program. It also participates in the Meals on Wheels program,
bringing nutritional meals to housebound elderly and disabled
people in the area.

Furnace Mountain takes every opportunity to participate in the
local economy. Whenever possible, they purchase materials and
supplies from nearby businesses. From the beginning they have
employed local trades people and artisans to construct and
maintain their buildings and roads. In keeping with Buddhist

principles of nonviolence and the interdependence, moreover, th_
take care to avoid altering the natural setting or harming plants
and trees in the area.

Before Mara Genthner and Zen Master Dae Gak purchased it, the
Furnace Mountain property had been unoccupied for more than
twenty years. In the 1950s, former owners had drilled a natural gas
well to operate oil rigs. Nearby residents, who had been tapping into
the well for free energy for many years, assumed that the new
owners would put a stop to that. When a neighbor reluctantly asked
Zen Master Dae Gak when he would shut it off, he exclaimed, "Why
would we do that? It's not *our* natural gas." They have continued to
allow contiguous neighbors to share the well free of charge.

The stranger becomes the host.

10. **Zen Master Dae Gak and community in front of the Zen Buddhist
temple at Furnace Mountain, Kentucky, in the Daniel Boone National
Forest. About forty miles north is Cane Ridge, the site of the 1801 camp
meeting that sparked the Second Great Awakening.**

y introduction to religion in America, whether very short or very ong, must end inconclusively. There is no last word. But what better place to stop, for now, than here, with a vantage point that takes in both Cane Ridge and Furnace Mountain?

On one hand, separated by two centuries, they are worlds apart. How many Kentuckians in 1801 were familiar with Buddhism? How many, if any, at the Cane Ridge camp meeting had even heard of the Buddha, let alone Zen? For that matter, how many of those meditating at Furnace Mountain today know about Cane Ridge or eastern Kentucky's role in the Second Great Awakening?

On the other hand, as close as a "country mile," they are distant cousins. Like Cane Ridge, Furnace Mountain represents a rapidly growing frontier religious movement—this time, American Zen Buddhism. Like the Protestant revivalism of Cane Ridge, this movement draws new, uniquely American beliefs and practices from long-established religious traditions. Like Cane Ridge, Furnace Mountain is part of an increasingly popular religious movement that is emerging outside the mainstream, and as such it has sometimes been represented as a threat to American society and identity.

Cane Ridge and Furnace Mountain are radically different yet strikingly kindred. But their differences and kinships need not lead to a family feud among their descendents, as has so often been the case in these parts. Together they testify to the rich, teeming diversity of the American religious landscape, yesterday and today, even as they lead us to wonder what new things this wild land will bring forth tomorrow.

References

Introduction

Marty, Martin E. *The One and the Many: America's Struggle for the Common Good*. Cambridge, MA: Harvard University Press, 1997.

Chapter 1:   Local Landscapes

Beal, Timothy, and students in the Spring 2003 Senior Seminar in Religious Studies at Case Western Reserve University. "Case Pluralism Project." Of the 3,832 undergraduates enrolled that academic year, we surveyed 635. Of those, 288 (45.3%) were freshmen, 127 (20%) were sophomores, 131 (20.6%) were juniors, and 87 (13.7%) were seniors; 302 were female and 316 were male (17 did not specify). The database and reports are available at Digital Case, hdl.handle.net/2186/ksl:CasePluralismProject.

Dillard, Annie. "On Seeing." In *Pilgrim at Tinker Creek*. New York: Harper's Magazine Press, 1974.

Orsi, Robert A. "Introduction: Crossing the City Line." In *Gods of the City: Religion and the American Urban Landscape*, edited by Robert A. Orsi, 47. Bloomington: Indiana University Press, 1999. Challenging the strong trend in religious studies to ignore urban religion, Orsi and the other contributors to this book call for attention to "the complex, contradictory, polysemous range of religious practices and understandings" within their specific environmental and social-historical contexts.

ıless otherwise noted, all data comes from the *2001 American Religious Identification Survey (ARIS),* by Barry A. Kosmin, Egon Mayer, and Ariela Keysar at the Graduate Center of the City University of New York, December 2001, available at www.gc.cuny.edu/faculty/research_studies/aris.pdf. The random telephone survey included 50,281 American households in the continental United States. In my discussions of this data, I include Unitarian Universalism under Christianity rather than under "Other Religions." This adds a thirty-sixth form of Christianity and an extra .3% to that total.

Another important resource for mapping the religious diversity of the United States is the Pluralism Project, led by Diana L. Eck at Harvard University, www.pluralism.org. Their numbers draw primarily from the 2004 edition of the *Yearbook* and the 2004 World Almanac.

It is difficult to disentangle religious identity from ethnic identity. ARIS found that of the 5.3 million Americans who self-identify as Jewish, only 53 percent (2.83 million) identify with Judaism as a religion. ARIS's estimates for Jews and Muslims in the United States are conservative. The 2001 American Jewish Identification Survey estimates the Jewish population to be almost 6 million. Higher numbers are also often claimed for Muslims and other groups.

Beal, Timothy K. "The Phineas Priesthood and the White Supremacist Bible." In *Sanctified Aggression: Violent Legacies of Biblical, Jewish and Christian Vocabularies,* edited by Jonneke Bekkenkamp and Yvonne Sherwood. Sheffield: Continuum, 2004.

——— . *Roadside Religion: In Search of the Sacred, the Strange, and the Substance of Faith.* Boston: Beacon Press, 2005.

Dawkins, Richard. *The God Delusion.* Boston: Houghton Mifflin, 2006.

Durkheim, Émile. *The Elementary Forms of Religious Life.* Translated by Carol Cosman. New York: Oxford University Press, 2001.

Harris, Sam. *Letter to a Christian Nation.* New York: Knopf, 2006.

Hitchens, Christopher. *God Is Not Great: How Religion Poisons Everything.* New York: Hachette, 2007.

Linder, Eileen W. *Yearbook of American and Canadian Churches 2007.* Nashville: Abingdon, 2007.

Melton, J. G. "The Changing Scene of New Religious Movemen
    Social Compass 42 (1995): 265–76.

Prothero, Stephen. *Religious Literacy: What Every American Needs to
    Know about Religion—And Doesn't.* San Francisco: HarperOne, 200?

On NRM's see esp. Stephen J. Stein, *Communities of Dissent: A History of
    Alternative Religions in America* (New York: Oxford University Press,
    2003), to which this discussion is heavily indebted. See also Christopher
    Partridge, ed., *New Religions: A Guide: New Religious Movements,
    Sects and Alternative Spiritualities* (New York: Oxford University Press,
    2004); and The Religious Movements Homepage Project at The
    University of Virginia, etext.virginia.edu/relmov.

An excellent introduction to the rise of the Christian Right is the
    documentary film, *With God on Our Side: George W. Bush and the
    Rise of the Religious Right in America*, directed by Calvin Skaggs
    and David Van Taylor (Sundance Channel, 2004). Ed Dobson's
    comments on the Moral Majority's loss of its prophetic role are from
    an interview in this film.

Recent criticisms, by evangelical Christians, of evangelicalism's
    compromising relationship with political power include Gregory
    A. Boyd, *The Myth of a Christian Nation: How the Quest for Political
    Power Is Destroying the Church* (Grand Rapids, Mich.: Zondervan,
    2006) and Randall Balmer, *Thy Kingdom Come: How the Religious
    Right Distorts the Faith and Threatens America: An Evangelical's
    Lament* (New York: Basic Books, 2006). There is also a progressive
    political movement of evangelical Christians concerned especially
    with matters of social and economic justice (which they would argue
    must be the core of the Christian Gospel), represented by *Sojourners*
    magazine and Jim Wallis's *God's Politics: Why the Right Gets It
    Wrong and the Left Doesn't Get It* (San Francisco: HarperOne, 2005).

Chapter 3: Looking Back

The most helpful introduction to scholarship on American religious
    history is Catherine L. Albanese, *American Religious History:
    A Bibliographic Essay* (Washington: United States Bureau
    of Educational and Cultural Affairs, 2002), exchanges.state.gov/
    education/amstudy, to which this discussion is indebted.

Deloria, Vine, Jr. "Anthropologists and Other Friends." In *Custer
    Died for Your Sins: An Indian Manifesto.* New York: Macmillan,
    1969.

., Vine, Jr. "Completing the Theological Circle: Civil Religion in ~nerica." In *For This Land: Writings on Religion in America*. New York: Routledge, 1999.

~utschke, Dwight. "American Indians in California." In *Five Views: An Ethnic Historic Site Survey for California*. Sacramento: California Department of Parks and Recreation, Office of Historic Preservation, 1988, www.cr.nps.gov/history/online_books/5views/5views1e.htm.

Dwight, Timothy. *The Nature and Danger of Infidel Philosophy, exhibited in Two Discourses, to the Candidates for the Baccalaureate in Yale College, September 9th*. New Haven: Geo. Bunce, 1797; and London: Hurst, Button, and Chapman, 1799.

Finney, Charles Grandison. *Lectures on Revivals of Religion*. Boston: Crocker and Brewster, 1835.

Hudson, Winthrop S. "The American Context as an Area for Research in Black Church Studies." *Church History* 3 (1983): 159–70.

"John Smith and Powhatan Exchange Views, 1608," memory.loc .gov/learn/features/timeline/colonial/indians/exchange.htm.

Locke, John. *Two Treatises on Government*. Cambridge: Cambridge University Press, 1988.

Lugo, Luis. "Moved by the Spirit: Pentecostal Power & Politics after 100 Years." Keynote address, conference at the University of Southern California, April 24, 2006.

Mayhew, Jonathan. *A Discourse Concerning Unlimited Submission and Non-Resistance to the Higher Powers with some Reflections on the Resistance made to King Charles the 1, and on the Anniversary of his Death, Published at the Request of His Hearers by Jonathan Mayhew* (1750).

McPherson, Aimee Semple. *This Is That*. Los Angeles: International Church of the Foursquare Gospel, 1923.

Rogers, Darrin J. "The Place of Azusa Street in Pentecostal Origins." In *Yearbook of American and Canadian Churches*, edited by Eileen W. Linder. Nashville: Abingdon Press, 2007.

Thornton, Russell. *American Indian Holocaust and Survival: A Population History Since 1492*. Norman: University of Oklahoma Press, 1987.

Trollope, Frances. *Domestic Manners of the Americans*. London, 1832.

Williams, Roger. *The Bloody Tenet of Persecution for Cause of Conscience Discussed in a Conference Between Truth and Peace*. London, 1644.

Zinn, Howard, and Anthony Arnove, eds. "Bartolemé de Las Casa
Two Readings on the Legacy of Christopher Columbus." In *Voice.
a People's History of the United States*. New York: Seven Stories
Press, 2004.

———— . "The *Diario* of Christopher Columbus (October 11–15, 1492)."
In *Voices of a People's History of the United States*. New York: Seven
Stories Press, 2004. The entry I quote is actually dated October 11,
but it must have been made on October 12.

Chapter 4: Looking Ahead

Adorno, Theodor. *Culture Industry*. London: Routledge, 1991.

Beal, Timothy. *The End of the Word As We Know It*. New York:
Harcourt, forthcoming.

Castells, Manuel. *The Rise of the Network Society*. Vol. 1 of *The
Information Age: Economy, Society and Culture*. Oxford:
Blackwell, 2000.

Eck, Diana L. *A New Religious America: How a "Christian Country"
Has Become the World's Most Religiously Diverse Nation*. San
Francisco: HarperSanFrancisco, 2001.

Lessig, Lawrence. *Free Culture: How Big Media Uses Technology
and the Law to Lock Down Culture and Control Creativity*.
www.free-culture.cc.

Miller, Vincent J. *Consuming Religion: Christian Faith and Practice in
a Consumer Culture*. New York: Continuum, 2004.

Data on Internet access among Americans comes from the National
Technology Scan, March 2007, conducted by Park Associates,
Dallas, Texas, www.parkassociates.com.

U. S. Census Bureau. "U.S. Interim Projections by Age, Sex, Race, and
Hispanic Origin." March 2004. www.census.gov/ipc/www/
usinterimproj/.

Warren, Rick, *The Purpose-Driven Life: What on Earth Am I Here For?*
Grand Rapids, MI: Zondervan, 2002.

Wosh, Peter J. *Spreading the Word: The Bible Business in Nineteenth-
Century America*. Ithaca, NY: Cornell University Press, 1994.

Chapter 5: To Coin a Phrase

Lévy, Bernard-Henri. *American Vertigo: Traveling America in the
Footsteps of Tocqueville*. New York: Random House, 2006.

Tocqueville, Alexis de. *Democracy in America*. Translated by Gerald
E. Bevan. New York: Penguin, 2003.

arther Reading

Albanese, Catherine L. *America: Religions and Religion*. Belmont: Wadsworth, 2006.

Balmer, Randall. *Mine Eyes Have Seen the Glory: A Journey into the Evangelical Subculture in America*. New York: Oxford University Press, 2006.

Beal, Timothy K., and Tod Linafelt, eds. *Mel Gibson's Bible: Religion, Popular Culture, and The Passion of the Christ*. Chicago: University of Chicago Press, 2006.

Bellah, Robert N., Richard Madsen, William M. Sullivan, Ann Swidler, and Steven M. Tipton. *Habits of the Heart: Individualism and Commitment in American Life*. Berkeley: University of California Press, 2007.

Butler, Jon, Grant Wacker, and Randall Balmer. *Religion in American Life: A Short History*. New York: Oxford University Press, 2002.

Castells, Manuel. "Epilogue: Informationalism and the Network Society." In *The Hacker Ethic: A Radical Approach to the Philosophy of Business*, by Pekka Himanen. New York: Random House, 2001.

Chidester, David. *Authentic Fakes: Religion and American Popular Culture*. Berkeley: University of California Press, 2005.

Cox, Harvey. *Fire from Heaven: The Rise of Pentecostal Spirituality and the Reshaping of Religion in the 21st Century*. New York: Da Capo Press, 2001.

Eck, Diana L. *A New Religious America: How a "Christian Country" Has Become the World's Most Religiously Diverse Nation*. San Francisco: HarperSanFrancisco, 2001.

Griffith, R. Marie. *American Religions: A Documentary History*. New York: Oxford University Press, 2007.

Keller, Rosemary Skinner, and Rosemary Radford Ruether, eds. *Encyclopedia of Women and Religion in North America*. Bloomington: Indiana University Press, 2006.

Kosmin, Barry A., and Ariela Keysar. *Religion in a Free Market: Religious and Non-Religious Americans, Who, What, Why, Where*. Ithaca, NY: Paramount Market Publishing, Inc., 2006.

Lessig, Lawrence. *Free Culture: How Big Media Uses Technology and the Law to Lock Down Culture and Control Creativity*. Available as free download at www.free-culture.cc.

Marsden, George M. *Fundamentalism and American Culture*. New York: Oxford University Press, 2006.

Marty, Martin E. *The One and the Many: America's Struggle for the Common Good*. Cambridge: Harvard University Press, 1997.

——. *Pilgrims in Their Own Land: 500 Years of Religion in America*. New York: Penguin, 1985.

Miller, Vincent J. *Consuming Religion: Christian Faith and Practice in a Consumer Culture*. New York: Continuum, 2004.

Moore, R. Laurence. *Religious Outsiders and the Making of Americans*. New York: Oxford University Press, 1985.

Morgan, David, and Sally M. Promney, eds. *The Visual Culture of American Religions*. Berkeley: University of California Press, 2001.

Neusner, Jacob, ed. *World Religions in America: An Introduction*. Louisville, KY: Westminster John Knox, 2003.

Noll, Mark A. *A History of Christianity in the United States and Canada*. Grand Rapids, MI: Eerdmans, 1992.

Orsi, Robert A., ed. *Gods of the City: Religion and the American Urban Landscape*. Bloomington: Indiana University Press, 1999.

Plate, S. Brent. *Blasphemy: Art that Offends*. London: Black Dog, 2006.

Prothero, Stephen. *American Jesus: How the Son of God Became a National Icon*. New York: Farrar, Straus, and Giroux, 2004.

Raboteau, Albert J. *African-American Religion*. New York: Oxford University Press, 1999.

Raphael, Marc Lee. *Judaism in America*. New York: Columbia University Press, 2003.

Sarna, Jonathan D. *American Judaism: A History*. New Haven: Yale University Press, 2005.

Seager, Richard Hughes. *Buddhism in America*. New York: Columbia University Press, 2000.

., Jonathan Z. "The Devil in Mr. Jones." In *Imagining Religion: From Babylon to Jonestown*. Chicago: University of Chicago Press, 1988.

Tweed, Thomas A., and Stephen Prothero. *Asian Religions in America: A Documentary History*. New York: Oxford University Press, 1998.

West, Cornel, and Eddie S. Glaude Jr., eds. *African American Religious Thought: An Anthology*. Louisville, KY: Westminster John Knox, 2003.

Index

Visit the
VERY SHORT
INTRODUCTIONS
Web Sites

www.oup.com/uk/vsi
www.oup.com/us

➤ **Information** about all published titles

➤ News of **forthcoming books**

➤ **Extracts** from the books, including titles
not yet published

➤ **Reviews** and views

➤ **Links** to other **web sites** and main OUP
web page

➤ Information about **VSIs in translation**

➤ **Contact** the editors

➤ **Order** other **VSIs** on-line

and your collection of

RY SHORT INTRODUCTIONS